Reaching Teenagers: Learning Centers for the Secondary Classroom

GOODYEAR EDUCATION SERIES
Theodore W. Hipple, Editor
University of South Carolina at Spartanburg

CHANGE FOR CHILDREN
Sandra N. Kaplan, Jo Ann B. Kaplan, Sheila K. Madsen, Bette K. Taylor

CREATING A LEARNING ENVIRONMENT
Ethel Breyfogle, Pamela Santich, Ronald Kremer, Susan Nelson, Carol Pitts

DO YOU READ ME?
Arnold Griese

IMAGINE THAT!
Joyce King and Carol Katzman

THE LANGUAGE ARTS IDEA BOOK
Joanne D. Schaff

THE LEARNING CENTER BOOK
Tom Davidson, Phyllis Fountain, Rachel Grogan, Verl Short, Judy Steely,
Katherine Freeman

LOVING AND BEYOND
Joe Abruscato and Jack Hassard

MAINSTREAMING LANGUAGE ARTS AND SOCIAL STUDIES
Charles R. Coble, Anne Adams, Paul B. Hounshell

MAINSTREAMING SCIENCE AND MATH
Charles R. Coble, Anne Adams, Paul B. Hounshell

NEW SCHOOLS FOR A NEW AGE
William Georgiades, Reuben Hilde, Grant Macaulay

ONE AT A TIME ALL AT ONCE
Jack E. Blackburn and Conrad Powell

THE OTHER SIDE OF THE REPORT CARD
Larry Chase

AN OUNCE OF PREVENTION PLUS A POUND OF CURE
Ronald W. Bruton

REACHING TEENAGERS
Don M. Beach

THE READING CORNER
Harry W. Forgan

A SURVIVAL KIT FOR TEACHERS AND PARENTS
Myrtle T. Collins and DWane R. Collins

THE WHOLE COSMOS CATALOG OF SCIENCE ACTIVITIES
Joe Abruscato and Jack Hassard

WILL THE REAL TEACHER PLEASE STAND UP? 2nd edition
Mary C. Greer and Bonnie Rubinstein

A YOUNG CHILD EXPERIENCES
Sandra N. Kaplan, Jo Ann B. Kaplan, Sheila K. Madsen, Bette K. Gould

Reaching Teenagers: Learning Centers for the Secondary Classroom

Don M. Beach, Ph.D.
The University of Texas at Arlington

Illustrations by Patricia Cox

Goodyear Publishing Company, Inc.
Santa Monica, California

For Linda, Blanche, Kathy,
and all creative teachers

Library of Congress Cataloging in Publication Data

Beach, Don M
  Reaching teenagers.

  (Goodyear education series)
  1. Open plan schools. 2. Creating thinking (Education) I. Title.
LB1029.06B42   373.1'3   76-40778
ISBN 0-87620-806-5
ISBN 0-87620-805-7 pbk.

Y-8057-5 (paper)
Y-8065-8 (case)
Current Printing (last digit):
10 9 8 7 6 5 4 3 2 1

Printed in the United States of America

Text and cover design: Linda Sanford Philips
Production editor: Janice Gallagher
Copy editor: Jackie Estrada

Contents

Preface

The call for the reform of secondary education has been made and documented extensively in recent years. Secondary schools are beginning to enroll students who have been through an elementary program built on learning centers, and teachers are beginning to ask, "How can we develop a learning center approach for the secondary classroom?"

This book is the result of several years of working with teachers in workshops, with student teachers in the public school setting, and with secondary-method students who are seeking ways to help students learn. Each learning center described here has been tried in a public school classroom and has met with success. The ideas for the learning center units and center activities are not wholly original. They are the result of working with teachers, both preservice and inservice, to bring about a learning center approach in a classroom. I am indebted to many students and teachers for their ideas and encouragement.

The activities in this book are designed to provide a guide for the teacher wishing to implement learning centers in the secondary classroom. The text provides a step-by-step explanation of the mechanics of building a center, selecting the activity to go in the center, and evaluating learning outcomes.

The key to the success of any program is the commitment and dedication of the classroom teacher, and it is no different for learning centers. The units and activities outlined in this book may need to be modified to fit specific situations, in which the teacher knows the interests and abilities of the students in the class. The learning centers are designed so that they can be modified by creative teachers who want to make learning centers work in their classrooms.

The success that I have had in working with individuals to develop learning centers in a secondary setting has prompted the desire to share ideas and activities with others. I hope the following pages will provide the necessary information to help teachers implement needed changes in the secondary school program.

Introduction

A learning center is an activity designed to teach a part of the subject-area curriculum. It is an area in the classroom where individual or small groups of students can go to work on a specific objective of the unit being studied. A learning center has two basic requirements, then: an activity specifically designed to promote learning, and an area or place where the directions for the activity are given and perhaps the task performed.

Learning centers vary according to their purpose. They may be designed to

1. teach a specific skill, such as preparing a microscope slide
2. stress the development of thinking and the learning processes, such as through a creative writing activity
3. employ topics, techniques, and tools to capture the student's enthusiasm and motivate him or her to participate in learning, such as by listening to a cassette tape or viewing a filmstrip

The centers should be designed to create direct sensory experiences to which words and ideas can be attached and through which concepts can be learned or clarified and the skills of "learning to learn" can be developed.

Each learning center should have activities designed to meet the needs of students at different levels. Within a unit, a variety of activities should be provided so that not all centers require the same kind of activity, such as reading an article or chapter and answering questions.

Centers can be set up in any area of the classroom or building. Some may be displayed on tables or on groups of desks put together, while others may be on the walls, on bulletin boards, on the floor, or even on the back of a cabinet door. The arrangement should allow individual students as well as small groups of students to work at the center.

A classroom could contain any number of learning centers. Some centers might be used to reinforce material that has been presented in the textbook or in class lectures, while others may be used to teach the entire unit of study. It is often helpful to begin with one to three centers and then move into a more individualized program, with more learning centers available.

When used in a classroom where the proper routine and ground rules have been established, learning centers can be one of the most effective teaching strategies in the secondary school.

1

Using Learning Centers in Secondary Classrooms

Why Use Learning Centers?

1. Learning centers are used to maximize the process of individualizing the curriculum to meet the needs and abilities of the students: to reach teenagers.

2. Learning centers allow students the opportunity to discover, explore, and investigate further those areas of knowledge that are of interest to them and, as a result, to remain occupied and advance further than students who have not been given a choice in selecting learning activities.

3. Learning centers provide opportunity for success and reinforcement in content areas, thereby encouraging learners to pursue the topic further and discover the unknown.

4. Studies (such as those of Piaget) indicate that students learn only what they are ready to learn. The center approach allows this concept to become effective in the classroom by providing options tied to readiness to learn.

5. Studies also indicate that no two learners come to school with the same knowledge or experiences. Therefore, teachers can provide for these differences through the use of learning centers.

6. The opportunity to choose their learning activities within a given content unit will help students become responsible decision makers.

Food for Thought:
It is just as incorrect to think that all tenth-grade boys should learn the same material in the same way at the same time as it is to think that they should wear the same size clothes.

Where Are Learning Centers Used?

1. Any teacher in any school facility can use learning centers in his or her teaching methodology. Schools with flexible or open spaces provide the most obvious situations in which learning centers can be established as an integral part of the educational program. The open-space area centered around a library or media center allows for more flexibility, and therefore more student-directed activities are possible.
2. Team teaching lends itself well to the learning center approach. The pooling of resources among teachers can produce imaginative and interesting centers. When teachers are responsible for their speciality, their imagination can run wild, and learning centers that develop from such an environment can be excellent. Furthermore, the classroom organization of students in a team-teaching setting lends itself to the learning center approach.
3. The establishment of centers in a secondary classroom that is traditionally self-contained can be most effective. The teacher can structure the learning environment and set up centers in a way that will meet the needs and interests of the students in that classroom for that period of the day. The teacher can establish a unique educational system within the walls of the classroom.
4. Learning centers can be used on a school-wide basis for mini-courses or on an individual basis in the classroom, but they will work only if individual teachers are committed to making them work. The key to success is to "dare to be different."

When Are Learning Centers Used?

1. One of the best ways to move into "centering learning" is to use a portion of each class period for center work. Perhaps while the teacher works with a small group of students another group can be working on an assignment at their desks and other students can work at the centers. The groups could even be rotated on a schedule so that each week every student would have an opportunity to work at the centers, have a small group discussion with the teacher, and work on an assignment. It might take two weeks to complete the cycle.
2. Teachers should allow enough time at the centers so that they are not viewed as a way of making "homework" assignments.

A teacher should make sure each student has the opportunity to go to the required centers for an adequate amount of time.

3. As the teacher and the students become accustomed to the new routine, more centers can be added to allow for more areas of the curriculum and more individualization of instruction. With each new center, student interests and needs can be incorporated into the learning process. When the routine becomes established, a fixed rotation schedule may no longer be needed.

4. In secondary classrooms, many students will want to design and implement their own learning centers. What more could a teacher ask than to have students ask permission to develop a center on Japanese Haiku while the the class is studying a unit on poetry?

5. The learning center approach can be used at any time with any content at the secondary level. Every subject in the secondary curriculum can be adapted to the learning center format with a little effort and some creativity.

How Are Learning Centers Set Up?

1. A learning center should provide the materials the students need to do the activities at the center (with the exception of routine writing materials).

2. Centers should also contain activities that challenge many learners. The activities provided should be designed for learners with different levels of knowledge and ability as well as with diverse interests.

3. The teacher should obtain all resource material and equipment in advance or should provide specific directions for obtaining the material or equipment.

4. The teacher should decide on specific objectives for the content in the curriculum and incorporate these objectives in the learning activities to be used in the centers. These activities should be presented in an interesting and graphic manner.

5. The students usually work in the center at their own rates and at their own level (unless the teacher has prescribed a rate and level), and they should be encouraged to try different levels.
6. The learning centers that involve factual content material should provide some type of self-corrective device so that students can receive immediate reinforcement for their responses.

Suggestion:
Learning centers are most effective when students are given the opportunity to make choices regarding their learning activities and to achieve and feel successful.

2

Developing Learning Centers

Steps in Developing Learning Centers

Comprehensive planning is needed to develop and implement learning centers in the classroom. Once a unit has been decided upon, the content and skills for the unit should be stated as objectives. The objectives then form the basis for learning activities at the centers, and the students should know exactly what is expected of them after having completed the activity at the center. It is often helpful to have a statement of the objective at the center, such as:

> After completing the activities at this center you should be able to name the twelve major parts of the microscope, prepare a microscope slide properly, and put the slide on the microscope and bring the specimen into focus.

After deciding upon the objectives for the unit, the teacher should select the activities that will teach the material to be mastered. Learning centers should include a variety of activities, and the activities within the center should be designed to bring success to all students and challenge the more advanced students. In selecting the activities the teacher should give attention to the abilities, interests, and needs of all the students in the class.

Successful learning centers utilize multi-media materials to teach the concept, support the topic, or reinforce the theme of the unit being studied. Such materials as slides, filmstrips, records, games, and posters can motivate students to participate in the center activity. The product of the activity is often in written form even though the activity itself may involve the student in watching, listening, or manipulating behavior that fosters exploration and discovery.

After the activities are selected, the directions to the students must be clearly written so as to establish a minimal need for the teacher to be present at the center. Directions are most effectively written when each step begins with an action or behavior. For example:

1. **Choose** one of the three short articles at the center.
2. **Read** the article quietly to yourself.
3. **Answer** the questions at the end of the article on the paper provided.
4. **Put** your answer sheet in the box at the center.

Finally, construct the center in the classroom. Use the back of a portable cabinet, bulletin boards within the room, cardboard boxes, or even the tops of desks or tables. A key factor for the success of the center will be the degree to which color and illustrations are used to "advertise" the center in the classroom. In developing a learning center unit the teacher should

1. select a topic or concept within the subject area assigned (for example, biology: mitosis; English: the short story; math: negative numbers; history: the Depression)
2. divide the topic or concept into major ideas to be learned, reinforced, applied, or evaluated
3. develop a learning center designed to teach the basic content or factual information of the unit
4. develop a learning center activity that would involve active participation from the student
5. develop an activity that would have the student apply previously learned information ·
6. develop a center that would have the student create a new product using information gained from the unit of study
7. develop evaluative criteria for each center
8. arrange the centers in the room to provide for students to use in a self-directed manner

Suppose then, that you are an English teacher with five classes of freshman English to teach. At the beginning of the year you have outlined the content, skills, and concepts that you will need to teach during the year. It is a continuous list that has been worked on by English teachers within your school system, and you are aware of the main points to be covered in your course as well as of what has been covered previously and what will be covered in the next three years.

You have decided that the unit you will teach using the learning center approach is a unit on the short story. Within that unit you have decided to teach

1. the major parts of a short story and how to identify those parts
2. the kinds of conflict often found in short stories and the ability to analyze the conflict
3. the titles and authors of at least three short stories to be read during the unit
4. the ability to write an original short story when given the raw ingredients of character, setting, and incidents

Realizing that each of these areas could form the basis of a learning center, you decide to develop your learning center unit around each concept or skill you want mastered within the unit.

Developing an English Learning Center Unit

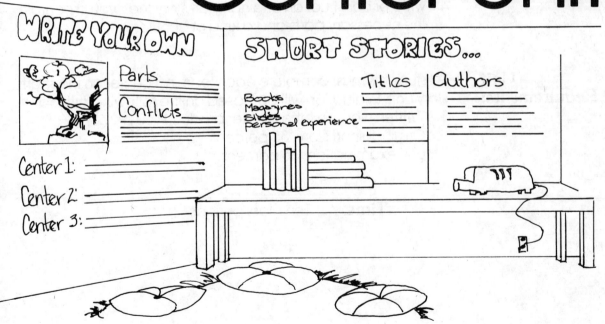

WRITE YOUR OWN

Parts_____

Conflicts_____

Center 1: _____
Center 2: _____
Center 3: _____

SHORT STORIES...

Books
Magazines
Slides
Personal experience

Titles | Authors

Unit: The Short Story

Concept:
The short story is a particular kind of literature with specific characteristics or parts.

Objectives:
After completing all of the learning centers the student should be able to
1. identify the parts of a short story
2. classify the kinds of conflict within a short story
3. identify the title and author of three short stories studied in class
4. write or construct an original short story that would contain the necessary parts and a kind of conflict

Unit Requirements:
All students must complete each learning center on the short story unit. Evaluation will be based on the following criteria:
1. Written work on other center products: 30 percent
2. Original short story: 35 percent
3. Unit examination: 35 percent

Time: Ten class periods.

10

Can You Identify the Parts of a Short Story?

Objective:

After completing the center the student should be able to identify the major parts of a short story by defining character, setting, and incident and by giving a brief synopsis of three short stories read, underlining each of the major parts.

Directions:

1. **Read** the definitions of each of the major parts of a short story.
2. **Select** three short stories to read from the list provided at the center.
3. **Read** all three short stories you have selected by the end of four days.
4. Using a 5 × 8 card for each story, **write** a brief description giving the characters, setting, and major incidents within each story.

Materials Teacher Provides:

The center should contain definitions of the major parts of a short story and a list of short stories approved for the unit. The list could be done in red, blue, and green, and the colors would indicate to the teacher the reading difficulty of the story.
The teacher should also provide the appropriate response sheets (5 × 8 cards).

CAN YOU IDENTIFY THE PARTS

OF A SHORT STORY?

SETTINGS	INCIDENTS

CHARACTERS

STORIES TO READ:	DIRECTIONS	COMPLETED WORK
_____	_____	
_____	_____	
_____	_____	
_____	_____	
_____	_____	
	_____	

Famous Short Stories

Center 2:

Objective:

After completing the center the student should be able to give the titles and authors of the short stories read in class and the title and author of the short story discussed in the film viewed in class.

Directions:

1. **Match** the title and author of each short story you have read in class, then make a chart of the major incidents in each.
2. **View** the film on the short story "The Necklace," and on your title and author list *record* the author and title of this short story.
3. **Listen** to one of the short stories recorded on cassette tape and **record** the title and author on your list.
4. **Place** your completed list in your folder.

Materials Teacher Provides:

The teacher should develop learning activities that will actively involve the student in the learning process. Here such active involvement would include operating a film projector and viewing a film, operating a cassette tape recorder and listening to a tape, and listing the titles and authors of the short stories. The teacher is therefore responsible for obtaining the appropriate films and tapes and the equipment to be used.

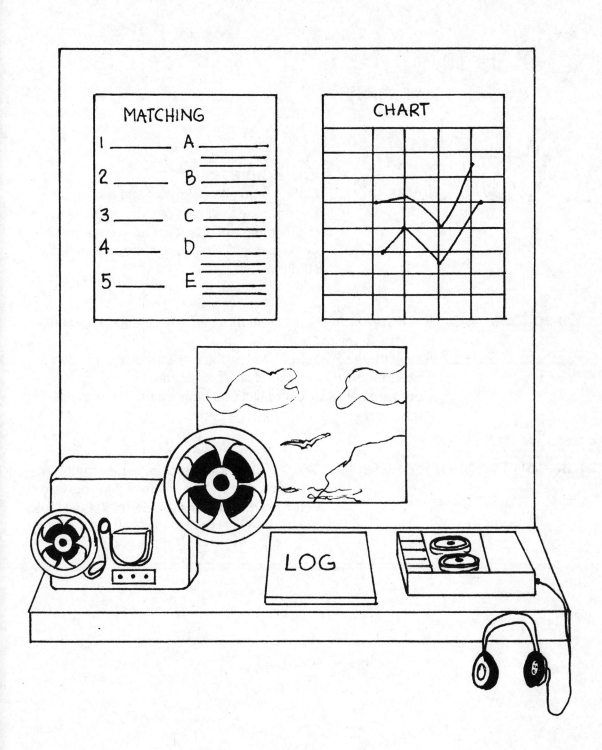

Compare the Kinds of Conflict

Center 3:

Objective:

Upon completion of the center the student will describe the kinds of conflict that occur in short stories and identify and compare the kinds of conflict in three of the short stories studied.

Directions:

1. **Read** the article at the center that discusses the kinds of conflict found in short stories.
2. **Select** three of the short stories you have read or studied in this unit and **identify** the kind of conflict described.
3. **Compare** the kinds of conflict you have identified from the three short stories in a two-page paper.

Materials Teacher Provides:

The teacher should provide a description of the kinds of conflict often found in short story writing. The teacher should provide examples of how conflict is evidenced in the short story.

AN APPLYING ACTIVITY

ILLUSTRATIONS

COMPARE

DIRECTIONS:

1. CONSIDER 3 SHORT STORIES READ IN UNIT.

2. COMPARE THE KINDS OF CONFLICT IN EACH —
MAN WITH MAN
MAN WITH NATURE
MAN WITH HIMSELF

3. SUBMIT COMPLETED PAPER TO TEACHER.

EXAMPLES

The ___

A ___

Man ___

See ___

Can You Write Your Own Short Story?

Center 4:

Objective:

Upon completion of the center the student will write an original short story based upon the characters, setting, incidents, and kind of conflict chosen.

Directions:

1. **Select** a CHARACTER card from the stack at the center.
2. **Select** a SETTING card from the stack at the center.
3. **Select** seven INCIDENT cards from the stack at the center.
4. Using the character(s), setting, and incidents you have selected, **decide** upon the most appropriate kind of conflict and **write** a short story based on the information you have selected.

Materials Teacher Provides:

The teacher should make a deck of character cards by writing such items as ''two teenage boys,'' ''a boy and his dog,'' ''two hunters,'' ''a housewife and a little boy,'' ''two policemen,'' ''a group of cheerleaders.'' The teacher should make a deck of setting cards with such locations as ''an abandoned hotel,'' ''a farming community,'' ''the university,'' ''school,'' ''home,'' ''a park.'' The teacher should make a deck of incident cards using such incidents as ''someone is lost,'' ''the lights go out,'' ''a gun is fired,'' ''a scream is heard,'' ''someone breaks a leg,'' ''it is snowing and thirty below zero.'' The decks of cards supply the raw ingredients for the original short stories.

Can you write your own short story?

| Character | + | Setting | + | Incidents | = |

Short Story

↓

FINISHED STORY

Putting It All Together

Gather all of the materials and activities for the four learning centers and arrange them in selected areas of the classroom to create "center areas" within the class. Remember to make your directions clear for students to use the centers in a self-directed manner. Centers should have large titles and illustrations that "advertise" the activity and catch the interest of the students. Be available to answer questions the first day as the students begin work in the learning centers.

Learning Center Planning Chart

Title of Unit: _____
Subject: _____
Concepts, themes, or goals: _____
_____
_____

Title of Center	Objective and Activity	Materials Needed

Design A Room Chart

Sketch your classroom as it might appear.

Checklist for Setting up Learning Center

__1. Are center activities based on clearly stated behavioral objectives taken from the course curriculum?

__2. Have you provided a chart that lists the procedures for working in the centers?

__3. Does each activity in the center have specific directions for accomplishing the learning tasks?

__4. Is the working space adequate for the activity that is planned?

__5. Are self-evaluation tools supplied for those activities that require immediate checking?

__6. Does the center include multi-level activities to meet the needs and abilities of students?

__7. Are center materials
__attractive to the eye?
__well arranged?
__challenging to students?
__coordinated around stated objectives?

21

3

Classroom Management and Learning Centers

Introducing Learning Centers to the Class

One of the easiest ways to introduce a unit designed around learning centers is to provide a sheet that explains the process and names the centers and the activity at each center. For example, the introduction to the unit on the short story might look something like:

Welcome to a classroom with new ways to learn!

The classroom has been set up with learning centers that contain the assignments and the topics of study for the next eight class periods. In order for us to learn and work together, some ground rules need to be established.

We will spend 45 minutes in the learning centers each day out of the 60 minute class period. The final part of the period will be spent discussing the various assignments at the centers, and group presentations can be made at this time.

We should avoid having more than five persons in most of the centers. If a center is full, return when a space becomes available.

Please replace items as you found them when you have finished at the center. If you have listened to a tape or seen a film, please rewind it so that the center is ready for the next person.

If you do not understand the directions, you may ask a friend to help you or ask the teacher for assistance. Budget your time carefully. Remember that you have only eight class periods in which to complete all of the assignments at the centers.

An introduction to the learning center approach should be followed by a brief discussion period so that the students have the opportunity to ask questions, so that additional guidelines can be set, and so that you can clarify any of the points that are vague to the students. Keep in mind that learning centers will be new to many of the students just as they may be new to you.

Establishing Guidelines

Although the introductory handout may help establish some general operating procedures, it may be necessary to be more specific in establishing operating guidelines. For example, how will you handle late material from the centers? Will all the material be turned in at the end of eight days, so that you will be swamped with papers to grade? What about examination requirements?

These are all valid questions that need to be answered in regard to the use of learning centers. Many answers only you can provide. You may wish to establish your own policy with regard to late work. In the matter of examinations, you may not wish to use unit examinations as a part of the evaluation process. Many of the suggested centers do not use a unit examination procedure. However, the use of learning centers does not preclude the use of unit examinations. The short story unit has a unit examination as a part of the total evaluation of the unit; it requires students to provide responses to key questions about the unit.

In order to help with the matter of grading papers or projects from the centers, many of the activities are self-correcting so that students can check themselves or have their peers check their papers. Classroom routine and scheduling are also helpful in dealing with the record-keeping problem.

Managing Classroom Routine and Scheduling

One of the most effective classroom routines is to have the students enter the classroom and begin working at the centers immediately. If you notice that one of the students is not working well at a center one day, meet that student at the door the next day and ask whether you can be of assistance in helping him get started. Perhaps you can suggest a center with which to begin the period.

Within an hour class period, it is often helpful to have 10 to 15 minutes at the end of the period for group discussion or a wrap-up session. Learning centers should not preclude group discussion, project presentations, or perhaps even a presentation by the teacher. Students learn from one another and it might be a good time to clarify questions about center activities or to get in an "advertisement" about one of the centers that is not being used.

A portion of the class period should be set aside for you to work with small groups of students if you wish. On Monday, for example, you might ask those students who are really doing well with the material to meet with you and discuss an enrichment topic for the unit. On Tuesday and Wednesday you might like to work with two small groups of students who are having difficulty doing the work because of a lack of motivation or ability. At these times reading abilities, verbal skills, and general aptitude for the subject could be assessed. On Thursdays and Fridays you could meet for a few minutes with other members of the class in small groups to have a general discussion of the topics and activities of the unit.

Finally, 20 to 30 minutes should be spent in circulating in the classroom to assist students at the centers, to answer questions, and to be actively involved in the learning process with the students. It is during this time period each day that you can begin to assess the progress each student is making in the unit. You will be able to detect whether a student is spending most of the time talking with a friend and not accomplishing the objectives of the unit. You can also make note of which students have been to the different centers, and during the discussion period at the end of the class period you can say, "Johnny, tell about the short story you read in the center today." This provides an opportunity to involve everyone in the classroom discussion.

While you are working with students in the centers, you might find it helpful to carry 3 × 5 cards to help you make notes to yourself, so that you can follow up on a student not doing his work or remember who was where in the learning centers that day. Such a system of note taking will help you remember to praise work of an exceptional nature or remind you to assist those students having problems.

4

Learning Centers for the Content Areas: Some Ready-Made Ideas

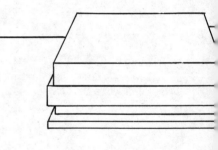

English and Language Arts

DICTIONARY

Nouns are _____

Unit: Imagery in Poetry

Concept:
An image in literature is a word or phrase that evokes a response in readers by appealing to one or more of their five senses. It therefore arouses readers physically and mentally.

Objectives:
After completing all of the assigned centers the student should be able to
1. construct sentences using words that would appeal to one or more of the senses
2. write a composition, describing a picture, that would use words that appeal to the senses
3. copy the lyrics to a contemporary song and identify the words that appeal to the senses

Unit Requirements:
All students must complete learning centers 1, 2, and 3 and do either learning center 4 or 5. Evaluation will be based on the following criteria:
1. Sentences using sensory words: 20 percent
2. Composition using descriptive, sensory words: 40 percent
3. Lyrics with sensory appealing words: 20 percent
4. Description of articles or poem illustration: 20 percent

Time: Seven class periods.

USE YOUR SENSES

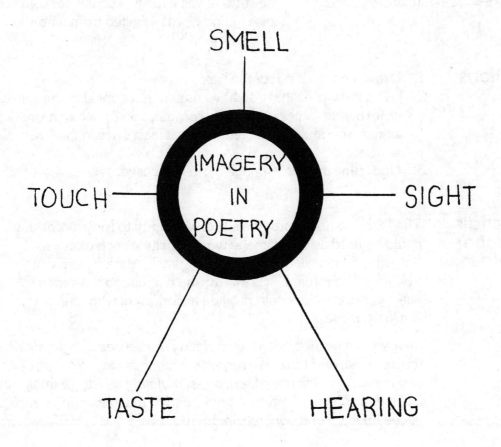

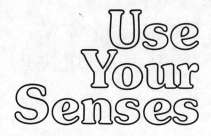
Use Your Senses

Center 1:

Objective:
The student will write five sentences using ten sense image words selected from a box.

Directions:

1. **Draw** ten words out of the box.
2. Using the words that you have drawn that appeal to the senses, **write** five sentences using any combination of two or more words. You must use all ten words at least once in the five sentences.
3. **Underline** the sense image words you used.

Materials Teacher Provides:

The teacher should provide a box with thirty to forty words that could be used as sense image words. Include such words as "buzzing," "crackling," "soft," "velvety," "dark," "brilliant," "blazing," "chortling." As a warm-up exercise to the center activity, the teacher could provide a worksheet with directions similar to these:

Imagery is a result of words stimulating our senses of sight, hearing, touch, smell, and taste. We respond in various ways both physically and mentally to the use of sensory-stimulating words, or imagery. Look through your literature books and find two examples each of vague imagery and concrete imagery.

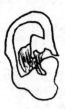

USE YOUR SENSES

DIRECTIONS:

Draw 10 words from the box that appeal to the senses. Using the words you have drawn, write 5 sentences using those words, to create images. Underline the image words in the sentence.

EXAMPLE:

<u>Cold</u> hands in <u>furry</u> mittens snuggled around the <u>crackling</u> <u>warmth</u> of the fire bring back memories of you.

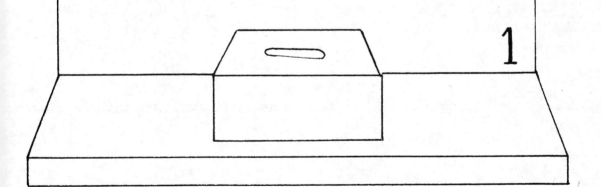

1

Picture This

Center 2:

Objective:

The student will write a two-page composition giving an impression of one of the pictures at the center, using words that would create mental images of the picture.

Directions:
1. **Study** each picture at the center carefully.
2. **Select** the picture that appeals to you most.
3. **Write** a composition of at least two pages that would describe the picture for someone else, using words that create mental images and stimulate the senses.
4. **Place** your composition in your unit folder.

Materials Teacher Provides:

The center should contain either a large folder or a mounted group of pictures that range from food to a pastoral scene, to people, to cities, to pop art or abstract art.

PICTURE THIS

DIRECTIONS
_____
_____
_____

2

Sound Imagery Surrounds You

Center 3:

Objective:

After copying the lyrics to a contemporary song, the student will be able to identify those words in the lyrics that create mental images and appeal to one or more of the senses.

Directions:

1. **Select** a record from the stack of albums at the center, then **select** a song on the album to listen to.
2. **Listen** to your selection and **copy** the lyrics (words) as accurately as possible.
3. **Underline** those words in the lyrics that create a mental image by appealing to one or more of the senses.
4. **Place** your lyrics in your unit folder.

Materials Teacher Provides:

The teacher needs to provide a wide selection of contemporary music for students to select their lyrics from. Many students will volunteer to bring their own albums and this will add to the possible selections. A record player should also be provided at the center, preferably one that has earphones to reduce the noise level in the classroom.

Feelings

Objective:

Upon completion of the center the student will be able to create word pictures for objects touched but not seen.

Directions:

1. **Choose** a partner to work with you.
2. **Put** your hand through the opening at the center and **feel** all of the articles contained in the sack.
3. **Decide** how many objects there are in the sack and then **write** a description of each article you felt, without looking.
4. If you have trouble in coming up with sensory words that would describe the articles, **consult** the thesaurus.
5. **Have** your partner check your descriptions against the real objects.
6. **Place** your descriptions in your unit folder.

Materials Teacher Provides:

Within the sack at the back of the center, the teacher needs to provide the articles to be felt and described. Suggested articles would include a lemon, a Q-tip, a tennis ball or golf ball, a marble, a plastic flower, a piece of fur, and even a piece of sandpaper. To make the activity more creative, the description of the articles could be in the form of a poem.

FEELINGS

DIRECTIONS

PUT YOUR HANDS IN HERE

4

Poetry Corner

Center 5:

Objective:

The student will illustrate a favorite poem using material provided at the center.

Directions:

1. Using the books provided at the center or books from the library or home, **select** a favorite poem.
2. Using the materials provided at the center, **illustrate** your favorite poem so that by looking at the illustration, someone can tell what your poem is about.
3. **Place** your illustration and a copy of the poem in your unit folder.

Materials Teacher Provides:

The teacher should provide several anthologies of poetry that would contain both contemporary and classical poetry. Poetry that is representative of different ethnic groups should also be included. Art materials such as pastel chalk, watercolor pens, magazine illustrations, and construction paper should be provided at the center.

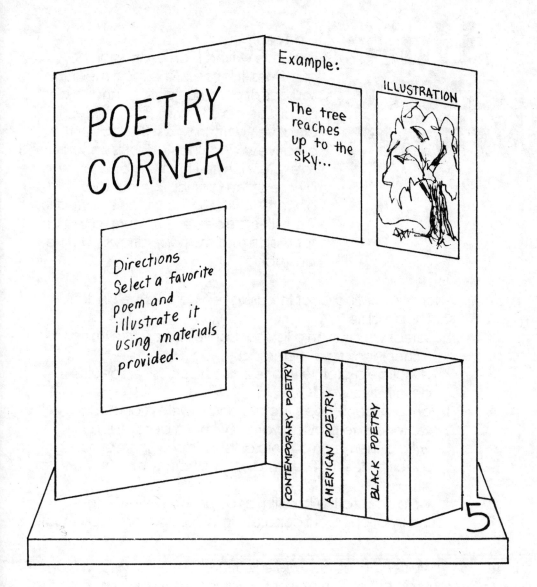

POETRY CORNER

Directions
Select a favorite poem and illustrate it using materials provided.

Example:

The tree reaches up to the sky...

ILLUSTRATION

CONTEMPORARY POETRY

AMERICAN POETRY

BLACK POETRY

5

Unit: Creative Writing

Concept:

Creative writing is an expression of ourselves. It is one of the most meaningful sources of communication, and students should be able to express their ideas in creatively written ways. By studying creative writing, the student is encouraged to express himself in writing and to become aware of the fact that an author's choice of words is vital to the idea he is creating. Activities are centered around a search for words that most specifically define an image.

Objectives:

After completing all of the assigned centers the student should be able to

1. select words from a list that convey a specific image rather than a general image
2. describe a picture in one paragraph using specific descriptive words
3. analyze sentence structure and rewrite monotonous sentences to provide variety within a paragraph
4. write a theme on a topic about himself, incorporating specific descriptive words and a variety of sentence structures
5. write a narrative to a film or a "police story" using information about concrete images and sentence structure

Unit Requirements:

All students must complete learning centers 1, 2, and 3 and must do either center 4 or 5. Evaluation will be based on the following criteria:

1. Learning Center 1: 20 percent
2. Learning Center 2: 20 percent
3. Learning Center 3: 30 percent
4. Learning Center 4 or 5: 30 percent

Time: Ten class periods.

EXPRESSING OURSELVES

Pictures and Words can help us build imagery!

Write a discriptive paragraph of the images you find in this picture.

Make a word list.

peaceful
primative
quiet
damp/cool
simple

Dictionary

Magazines

What Mental Picture Do These Words Conjure?

Center 1:

Objective:
Upon completion of the center the student should be able to select from a list of words those that create a specific mental image or description and, using descriptive words, write a paragraph about the witch pictured at the center.

Directions:
1. **Take** the pretest. If you miss no more than two, continue to Step 3. If you miss more than two, go to Step 2.
2. **Take** the two paragraphs from the pocket in the witch's caldron. **Read** each paragraph carefully. Which paragraph gives you the most vivid mental picture? **Write** down the words that are the most descriptive. **Compare** your list with others at the center.
3. **Look** at the witch on the poster. Can you describe her? **Make** a list of words that would describe the witch. You may use the thesaurus if you need to. Then **write** a paragraph that would describe the witch, using the words you have found that would create a mental image of her.
4. **Place** your description in the "Witch Description Box."

Materials Teacher Provides:
The teacher should provide the prestest form and the answers for checking the pretest. The teacher should also find two paragraphs, one that would create vivid images and one that would create vague, general images. These go in the witch's caldron. At least one thesaurus and a box to place the completed descriptions in should be provided.

Pretest:

Place a check by the words that create a definite image in your mind.

_____ 1. shaggy   _____ 6. shimmering
_____ 2. good   _____ 7. luminous
_____ 3. pungent   _____ 8. jagged
_____ 4. crackling   _____ 9. effervescent
_____ 5. happy   _____ 10. bad

Self-Check:

Those words that would most appropriately create definite images are: 1, 3, 4, 6, 7, 8, and 9.

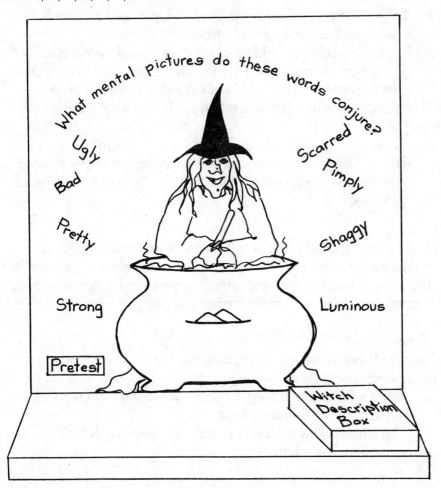

Variety is the Spice of Life

Center 2:

Objective:

After completing the center the student should be able to detect a monotonous sentence structure and to change sentences within a paragraph to provide variety of sentence structure.

Directions:

1. **Take** the pretest. If you miss only one, proceed to Step 3. If you miss more than one, go to Step 2.
2. From the pocket of unlabeled spice jars, **read** the six enclosed paragraphs. **Discuss** with the teacher or students at the center how the paragraphs could be changed to make them more interesting. When you feel you have found a solution, *go to* Step 3.
3. **Choose** two of the paragraphs and rewrite them using several different kinds of sentence structure. When you have finished rewriting the paragraphs, **place** them in the pocket of labeled spice jars.

Materials Teacher Provides:

The teacher should provide the pretest forms and suggested guidelines for checking them. The teacher should also provide (for the pocket of unlabeled spice jars), six paragraphs that are poorly written with no variety of sentence structure.

Pretest:

Rewrite these sentences combining them into compound or complex sentences:

1. It was a Saturday in May. Charley was fixing a flat on my bike. I ran into an old friend of mine.
2. The whistle blew for the end of the second quarter. The coach motioned Jake off the field.

3. Karen hurried across the gym. Her friends were waiting for her.
4. It was after chemistry class. Tom met me in the hall.
5. Mike turned the corner. He saw the bully. He ran.

Suggested Self-Check:
1. It was a Saturday in May and while Charley was fixing a flat on my bike, I ran into an old friend of mine.
2. The whistle blew for the end of the second quarter and the coach motioned Jake off the field.
3. Karen hurried across the gym because her friends were waiting for her.
4. It was after chemistry class when Tom met me in the hall.
5. As Mike turned the corner, he saw the bully and ran.

Do Your Own Thing

Center 3:

Objective:
The student will write a theme in class based on a topic about himself, using his own experiences.

Directions:

1. **Look** at the center of the flower to see the most interesting person you know. Now, **look** at the topics surrounding you and **proceed** to Step 2.
2. **Choose** one of the topics on the flower petals and **write** a one-page theme on that topic. You may create a story using your own experiences or describe the event and how you felt. Remember to use a variety of sentence structures and descriptive words.
3. **Leave** your finished paper in the box at the center.

Materials Teacher Provides:

The center should be constructed in such a way as to have a mirror at the center of the flower. Topics of personal interest for the students should form the petals of the flower.

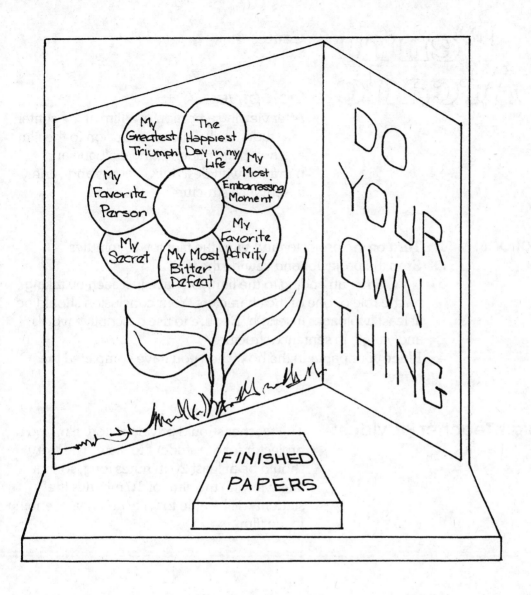

My Greatest Triumph

The Happiest Day in my Life

My Most Embarrassing Moment

My Favorite Person

My Favorite Activity

My Secret

My Most Bitter Defeat

DO YOUR OWN THING

FINISHED PAPERS

Penny Arcade

Center 4:

Objective:

After viewing a portion of a film at the center, the student will write a conclusion to the film in a two-page paper, using dialogue and narration with descriptive words and variety in sentence structure.

Directions:

1. **Turn on** the projector and **view** the film for 10 minutes.
2. **Stop** the projector and **rewind** the film.
3. Now, **write** an ending to the film you have just seen by taking on the role of one of the characters. Your conclusion should be at least two pages in length. Be sure to use descriptive words and variety in sentence structure.
4. **Place** your paper in the box when you have completed the center.

Materials Teacher Provides:

The teacher should privide a story film and a projector for the student to view. The story should be at least 20 minutes long, so that after viewing the film for 10 minutes the student will be able to write an original ending to the film.

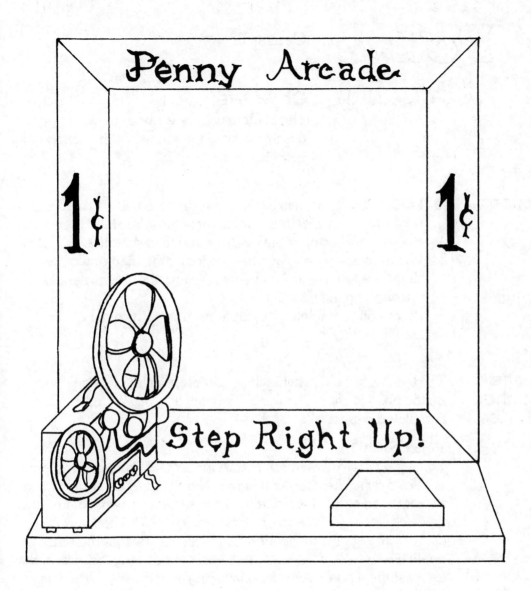

Police Story

Objective:

The student will write a one- to two-page description of a person within the context of a specific event.

Directions:

1. **Look** at the characters before you. In the lower left-hand pocket **take out** the events that involve these people. **Read** them carefully and **choose** the event you wish to describe.
2. **Write** a one- to two-page description of the man or woman you have selected, using the event given and the circumstances surrounding the event.
3. **Place** your completed descriptions in the "Criminal Identification Box."

Materials Teacher Provides:

The teacher should provide the situations that involve the people on the posters and a "Criminal Identification Box" for the completed papers.

Police Story 1

You are a jewelry store manager. A luscious-looking young woman ambles over to the counter where you pretend to be busily dusting the diamond case. She politely asks to see the stunning diamond bracelet that has just been appraised at $10,000. You lavishly display the scintillating diamond bracelet. As she tries the bracelet on, two rough-looking young men walk in decrying the evils of the establishment and the vanity of wanting jewelry. When they begin to insult the lovely creature you have been waiting on, your face blushes crimson, the veins in your neck bulge, and in a constrained whisper you hiss at the two men to leave the store.

The two young men leave the store and you sigh in relief. The lady says "Thank you," returns the bracelet, and leaves the store. You gaze at her lovely form until the door blocks her from view. You begin to return the bracelet to its display case when you notice the clasp is broken and several stones are missing. Suddenly you discover it's a fake. You've been duped. You run into the street, but she is nowhere in sight. The police arrive shortly thereafter and ask for an account and a detailed description of the lady.

Police Story 2

You are walking down the street when a man pulls a gun on you and forces you into an alley. He demands that you give him your pocketbook. You give him your wallet, which contains $50. He strips the money out of the wallet and then throws it out into the street. Not pleased with the take, he demands your watch, too. Hurriedly you remove the watch while he glares at you. He grabs the watch and runs. You hurry to the police station to file a report of the incident and give a description of the robber.

Police Story 3

You are on your way to the corner drugstore to meet some friends for a Coke when you are met by a dirty, unshaven man. "Hey, you want some kicks?" "What do you mean?" you ask. He reaches into his pocket and pulls out a handful of pills. You suspect these are dangerous drugs. You run to the drugstore and call the police to tell them about the "pusher" in the neighborhood. "Okay," says the metallic voice on the telephone, "tell me all about it and what he looked like."

Road Rally Vocabulary

Objective:
Upon completion of the center the student should be able to define all of the vocabulary words for the unit.

Directions:

1. **Select** two to four players for the game.
2. **Spin** the spinner. The spinner. The one who lands on green goes first.
3. First player spins the spinner. If it lands on red, one of the other players draws a word from the red deck and asks the first player to define it. If correct, he moves ahead one space. If a player lands on blue and answers correctly, he may move ahead two spaces. If a player lands on green, he may move ahead three spaces. If the definition is incorrect, the player loses that turn and makes no move. If a player lands on a shortcut space, he may choose from the red, blue, or green deck and if he answers correctly, he may move ahead the appropriate number of spaces. If a word from the shortcut turn is missed, the player must move back the number of spaces indicated by the color selected.

Materials Teacher Provides:

The teacher should provide the words, with the definitions on the back for the red, blue, and green decks. The teacher should also provide the game board and the spinner for determining moves.

ROAD RALLY VOCABULARY

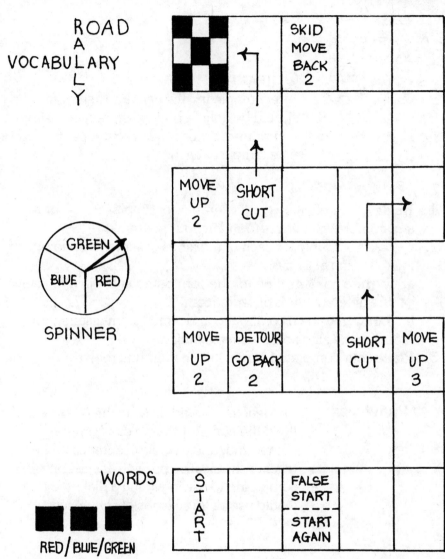

SPINNER

GREEN
BLUE   RED

WORDS

RED / BLUE / GREEN

SKID MOVE BACK 2

MOVE UP 2

SHORT CUT

MOVE UP 2

DETOUR GO BACK 2

SHORT CUT

MOVE UP 3

START

FALSE START

START AGAIN

What Do You Say?

Center Activity:

Objective:
After completing the center the student should be able to distinguish between simple, compound, and complex sentences and write an example of each.

Directions:
1. **Review** the definitions and examples of simple, compound, and complex sentences found in your textbook.
2. Using an example for each of the kinds of sentences, do one of the following activities:
   a. **Write** a conversation for the comic strip at the center using the different kinds of sentences.
   b. **Draw** your own comic strip and write a conversation for it using the kinds of sentences studied.
3. **Place** your completed comic strip in your unit folder.

Materials Teacher Provides:
The teacher should provide the references for the definition and examples of simple, compound, and complex sentences. The teacher should also provide at least one comic strip to use in writing a dialogue that would use all three kinds of sentences.

54

WHAT DO YOU SAY?

DIRECTIONS

1. REVIEW
2. CHOOSE

 OR

3. DRAW YOUR OWN COMIC STRIP AND WRITE A CONVERSATION FOR IT USING INFORMATION FROM STEPS 1 & 2.

4. WRITE A CONVERSATION FOR THE STRIP BELOW:

Get The Message

Center Activity:

Objective:
The student will demonstrate his awareness of the correlation of various means of communication by analyzing the relationships between two or more media.

Directions:

1. **Study** the picture at the center carefully. What does it say to you, if anything?
2. **Study** one of the poems. Does it relate to the picture? Why or why not?
3. **Read** the lyrics to the songs and **listen** to them on tape. How do they relate to the picture and the poem you selected? THINK IT OVER.
4. **Choose** one of the following and have fun:
   a. Compose a poem that the picture would illustrate.
   b. Sketch a picture to illustrate the poem you selected or to fit the lyrics to one of the songs.
   c. Write lyrics (and music if you can) to fit the picture.
   d. Write an essay responding to the questions asked about each part of the center (limit of two pages).
5. **Submit** the finished product to the teacher.

Materials Teacher Provides:

The teacher should select an appropriate picture for the center, lyrics to three or four contemporary songs (and cassette recordings if possible), several kinds of poems, and materials for sketching (if students have none).

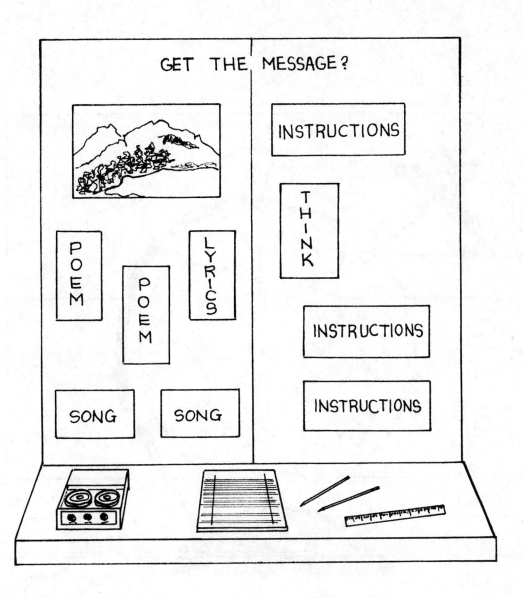

GET THE MESSAGE?

58

Social Studies, History, and Government

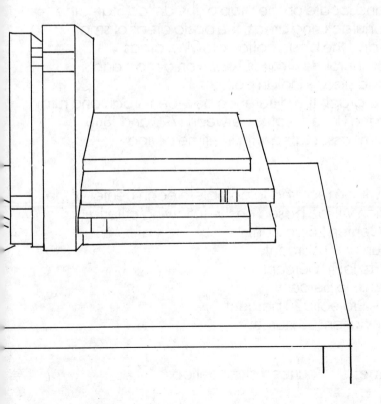

Unit: Jackson and the Wild West

Concept:
The Jacksonian Era was a period of great transition from the "old" ways of the past to the "modern times." Our present-day political parties were beginning to develop, and the participation of the "common man" in government started the feelings of American democracy. The Jacksonian Era is important in that it helps one to understand the political party system and the growth of "big business" and to examine Daniel Boone, Andrew Jackson, and other western heroes.

Objectives:

After completing the unit the student should be able to
1. name major people during the period of time and indicate their importance
2. identify and locate on the map of the United States the basic manufacturing areas, the basic areas of small farming, and the basic cotton growing areas
3. trace the Cherokee "Trail of Tears" on a map and describe Jackson's Indian policy
4. trace on a graph the difference between urban and rural growth in the United States between 1790 and 1840
5. define terms associated with the time period

Unit Requirements:

All students will be required to complete each center of the unit. Evaluation will be based on the following criteria:
1. Caucus Center: 25 percent
2. Atlas Country: 10 percent
3. Jigsaw Puzzle: 10 percent
4. Book Board: 15 percent
5. Wanted — Projects: 20 percent
6. Unit Examination: 20 percent

Time: Fourteen class periods.

60

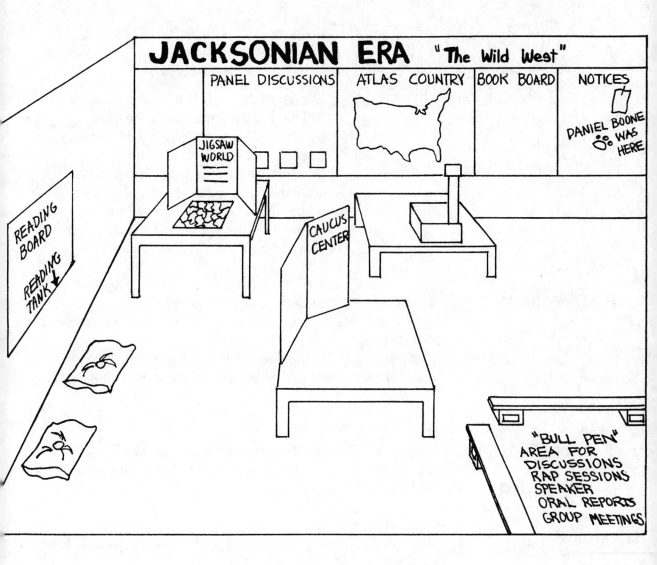

Caucus Center

Center 1:

Objective:

After completing the center the student should be able to discuss in writing Jackson's election to the presidency and the circumstances surrounding his election and administration. Such specific areas as popular rule, nominating conventions, political parties, and the Harrison-Tyler campaign should be covered in the discussion.

Directions:

1. **Read** the questions for discussion at the center.
2. **Consult** the reference books at the center or use the chapter in your textbook.
3. After thinking about the questions and discussing them with others at the center, **submit** your conclusions in writing to the teacher.

Materials Teacher Provides:

The teacher should provide several reference books that would address the issues raised at the center. The discussion topics should also be listed at the center.

Topics to Discuss:

1. Why was Jackson a popular president? How was he able to win the election in 1828?
2. Characterize the developments in the rule by the people.
3. Trace the development of nominating conventions. How do they work? Do they work the same today?
4. What were the differences between the Whig and Democratic parties?
5. Explain the significance of the Harrison-Tyler campaign.

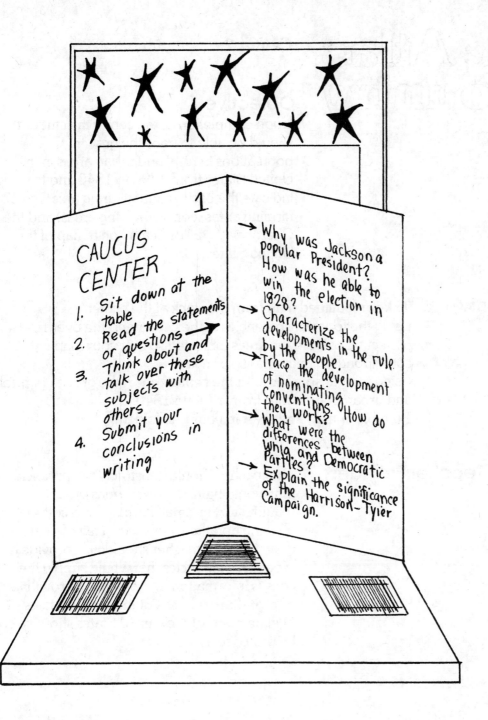

CAUCUS CENTER

1. Sit down at the table
2. Read the statements or questions
3. Think about and talk over these subjects with others
4. Submit your conclusions in writing

1

→ Why was Jackson a popular President? How was he able to win the election in 1828?

→ Characterize the developments in the rule by the people.

→ Trace the development of nominating conventions. How do they work?

→ What were the differences between Whig and Democratic Parties?

→ Explain the significance of the Harrison-Tyler Campaign.

The Atlas Country

Objective:

Upon completion of the center the student should be able to trace the growth of populations in rural and urban areas in the United States from 1790 to 1840 and to indicate the basic manufacturing areas, small farming areas, cotton growing areas, and the Cherokee "Trail of Tears" on a map of the United States.

Directions:

1. **Take** an outlined map from the stack at the center.
2. Using the four transparencies at the center and the overhead projector, **color** in the areas indicated so that your map corresponds with the transparencies.
3. Using the transparencies at the center, **chart** the growth of rural and urban populations from 1790 to 1840.
4. **Place** your map and chart in your unit folder.

Materials Teacher Provides:

The teacher should construct transparencies that would have the basic areas of manufacturing, small farming, and cotton growing and the Cherokee "Trail of Tears" drawn in. The teacher should also provide a set of transparencies that would supply the census information on population growth in rural and urban areas of the United States. Outline maps of the United States should also be provided.

The Atlas Country

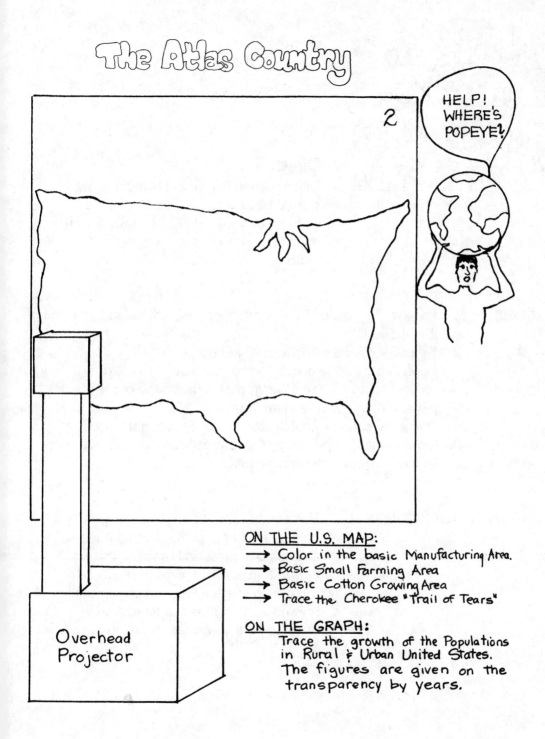

2

HELP! WHERE'S POPEYE!

ON THE U.S. MAP:
→ Color in the basic Manufacturing Area.
→ Basic Small Farming Area
→ Basic Cotton Growing Area
→ Trace the Cherokee "Trail of Tears"

ON THE GRAPH:
Trace the growth of the Populations in Rural & Urban United States. The figures are given on the transparency by years.

Overhead Projector

Jigsaw Puzzle — Match Me if You Can

Objective:

Upon completion of the center the student should be able to define terms associated with the period and give the names and explain the importance of people of the period.

Directions:

1. **Look** at the shape of the puzzle piece as outlined in the frame of the puzzle.
2. **Read** the question in the outlined shape.
3. **Look** at the puzzle pieces to find the answer to the question. If you do not know the answer, match the shape of the puzzle piece with the outline in the frame.
4. **Place** the correct puzzle piece on the appropriate question.
5. On a sheet of paper, **copy** the question and the answer, then **place** the paper in your unit folder.

Materials Teacher Provides:

The teacher should construct a jigsaw puzzle. Each piece of the puzzle should have an answer to a question regarding the time period. On another piece of poster board, trace each puzzle piece to form an outline of the shape. Within the outline, write a question to the answer on the puzzle piece.

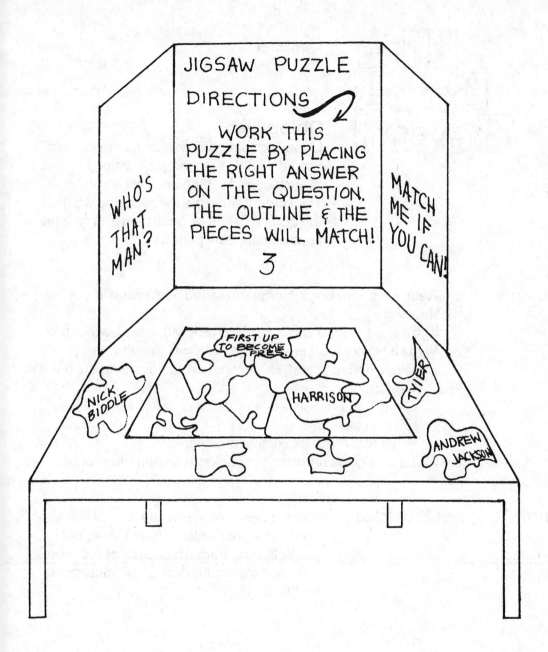

The
Book
Board

Center 4:

Objective:
Upon completion of the center the student should be able to discuss the action, character, and setting in a "western" book. The student should also determine whether the book is fiction or nonfiction and give the approximate time period.

Directions:

1. **Read** a western book. Some suggested titles found in our library are . . .
   If you want to read another title, check with your teacher first.
2. **Write** a book report answering the following questions:
   a. What kind of action, character, and setting made the book a western?
   b. Did the author use facts in a fictional or nonfictional way? Give an example.
   c. What was the approximate time period?
3. **Place** your book report in the pocket at the learning center.

Materials Teacher Provides:

The teacher should provide a list of western books that are available from the school or public library. Perhaps an area of the room designed for reading would be appropriate for the center.

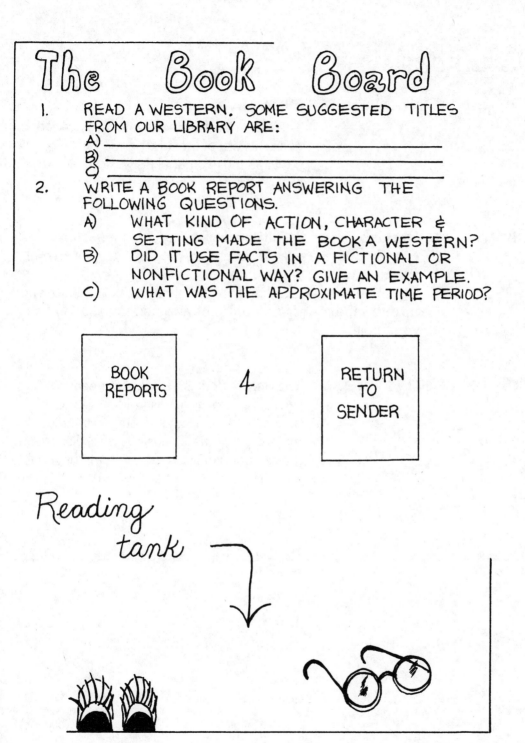

The Book Board

1. READ A WESTERN. SOME SUGGESTED TITLES FROM OUR LIBRARY ARE:
    A) _____
    B) _____
    C) _____

2. WRITE A BOOK REPORT ANSWERING THE FOLLOWING QUESTIONS.
    A) WHAT KIND OF ACTION, CHARACTER & SETTING MADE THE BOOK A WESTERN?
    B) DID IT USE FACTS IN A FICTIONAL OR NONFICTIONAL WAY? GIVE AN EXAMPLE.
    C) WHAT WAS THE APPROXIMATE TIME PERIOD?

BOOK REPORTS

4

RETURN TO SENDER

Reading tank

Wanted — Projects

Objective:

The student will demonstrate his knowledge of the history of the time period by participating in a panel discussion, giving an oral report, or performing a skit.

Directions:

1. **Decide** on a project that you would like to do for the unit. You can participate in a panel discussion, prepare and give an oral report, or write and perform a skit.
2. Once you have decided on the kind of project you will do, **sign up** under the correct category to be assigned a time to present your project.

Materials Teacher Provides:

The only materials the teacher needs to provide are a sign-up list under the various project categories and possible resource materials such as suggested panel discussion topics, oral report topics, or situations suitable for skits.

WANTED

PERSONS FOR: PANEL DISCUSSIONS
                         SKITS
                         ORAL REPORT

APPLY HERE

PANEL DISCUSSIONS

BANK   NULLIFICATION

SKITS

ORAL REPORT

Unit: The War Between The States

Concept:
A major portion of the history of the United States is devoted to the study of the war between the states. Students should be aware of the causes, the conflicts, the battles, and the implications of the war.

Objectives: After completing the unit the student should be able to
1. give the major reasons for the war between the states and discuss the implications of those reasons as they relate to regionalism in the United States today
2. discuss the battle strategies of both the North and the South, citing major battles and generals for each
3. provide a year-by-year description of the war and the major events of each year

Unit Requirements: Each student will complete all learning centers developed for the unit. Evaluation will be based on the following criteria:
1. War Correspondent Center: 30 percent
2. News From the Front Center: 30 percent
3. Fighting the War Center: 10 percent
4. Unit Exam: 30 percent

Time: Twelve class periods.

72

A COUNTRY DIVIDED

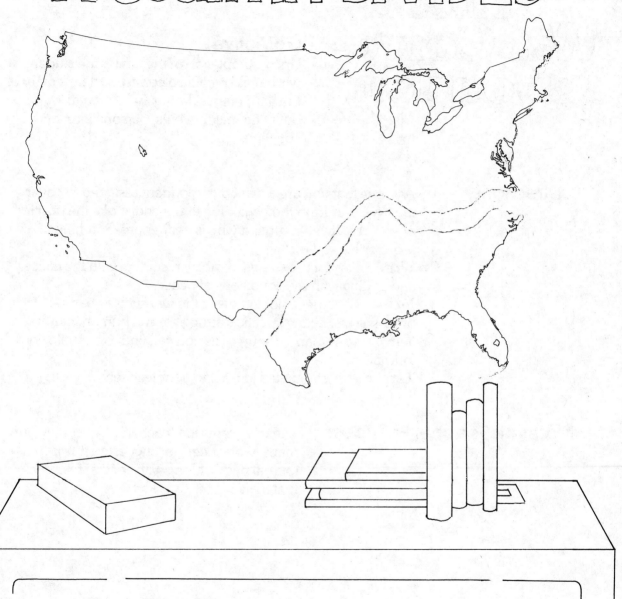

You Are There — War Correspondent Kit

Center 1:

Objective:
Upon completion of the center the student will have compiled a correspondent's diary of the happenings during the war years by outlining major events, personalities, and concerns.

Directions:

1. **Assume** that you are a war correspondent assigned to cover the Civil War from the beginning to the end. **Take** the position of an "objective" journalist who is neither pro-South nor pro-North.
2. **Write** a diary of the events of the war, starting with the causes and ending with the conditions of peace.
3. **Include** all of the major events of the war such as battles, personalities, events, political struggles, and human interest items. **Use** as many resources as you can find to compile your journal.
4. **Turn in** your completed journal to your teacher.

Materials Teacher Provides:

The only items the teacher might supply are maps, worksheets, or suggested forms for journal pages, along with several reference materials.

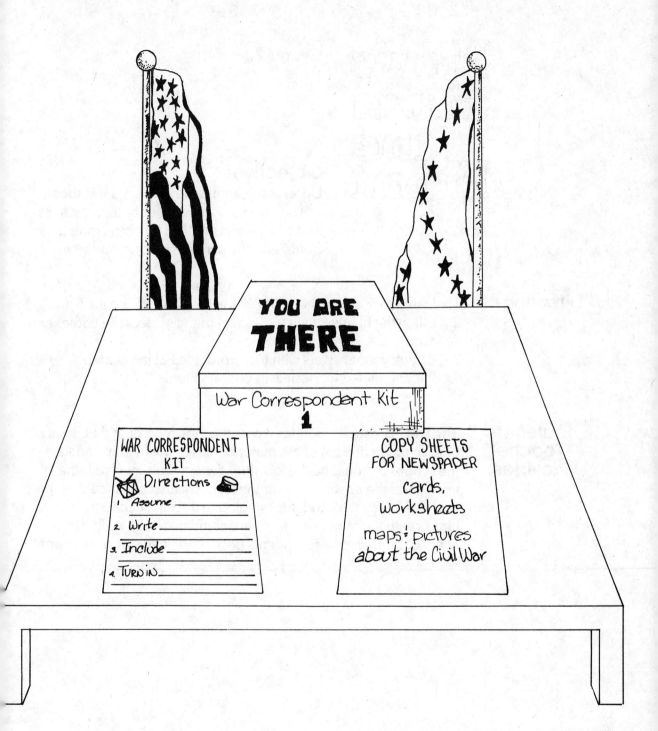

YOU ARE
THERE

War Correspondent Kit
1

WAR CORRESPONDENT
KIT
Directions
1. Assume _____
2. Write _____
3. Include _____
4. TURN IN _____

COPY SHEETS
FOR NEWSPAPER
cards,
worksheets
maps & pictures
about the Civil War

News From the Front

Objective:

Upon completion of the center the student will be able to discuss major battle strategies and battles won and lost by both North and South and the generals involved in each.

Directions:

1. **Listen** to the tape recording giving the "news from the front."
2. **Fill in** the blanks of the worksheet that discusses the battles and generals.
3. **Check** your answers with those provided at the center.
4. **Put** completed worksheet in your unit folder.

Materials Teacher Provides:

The teacher should produce a cassette tape recording that gives a brief synopsis of each of the major battles of the war. Included in the synopsis should be the location, the generals involved, the victor, and the implications for the war. The teacher should prepare a worksheet so that students listening to the tape can fill in the blanks with the major points. There could be a tape each day or every other day to keep students posted on "news from the front."

NEWS FROM THE FRONT

1. Listen _____
2. Fill _____
3. Check _____
4. Put Completed _____

2

Fighting the War

Objective:

After completing the center the student should be able to recall major facts concerning the war between the states and cite those facts when called upon.

Directions:

1. **Select** a playing token. **Determine** a procedure for establishing which player should go first.
2. The first player draws a question card. The question card will indicate the number of spaces to move forward if answered correctly. (The more difficult the question, the more spaces a player moves forward.) One of the opposing players asks the first player the question drawn, and if he answers correctly, he moves forward the number of spaces indicated. If he answers incorrectly, the question is placed on the bottom of the stack and he remains where he is. This procedure continues with each player.
3. The first player to reach "Finish" wins the game.

Materials Teacher Provides:

The teacher should construct the game board and make up the question deck using questions about content from the unit on the war between the states. Any object can be used for a game token. The easy questions should count for 1 space forward, the medium questions 2 spaces, and the difficult questions 3 spaces.

CONFIGURATION

DIRECTIONS:

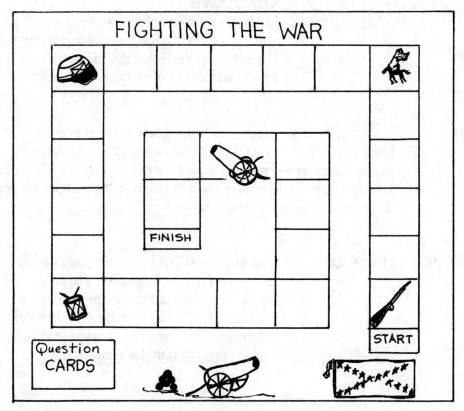

FIGHTING THE WAR

FINISH

START

Question CARDS

▲ ■ ● ♣
PLAYING TOKENS

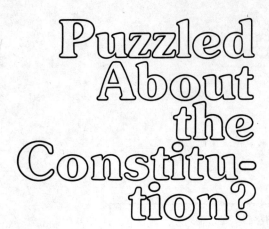

Puzzled About the Constitution?

Center Activity:

Objective:
Upon completion of the center the student will be able to discuss the major parts of the Constitution and state the major elements contained within each part.

Directions:
1. **Take** a crossword puzzle from the stack at the center.
2. Using your textbook and the other resources provided at the center, **answer** the questions and **work** the puzzle.
3. **Check** your puzzle answers with those provided at the center.
4. **Turn** your puzzle in to the teacher.

Materials Teacher Provides:
The teacher should provide copies of the crossword puzzle for students to use at the center. Any references on the Constitution, including textbooks, can be used in working the puzzle. An answer check sheet should also be provided at the center.

Crossword Puzzle on the Constitution

Across

1. The document that is composed of the Preamble, seven Articles, and the Amendments
4. The only court established by the Constitution (two words)
9. This word means a two-house legislative branch
11. What Representatives are apportioned according to
14. The branch that enforces laws
15. The Article that deals with the executive branch
19. The Article that deals with the judicial branch
20. The Amendment that deals with the Negroes' right to vote
22. What represents the people in Congress (three words)
29. This phrase means that a person cannot serve in more than one branch of government at the same time (three words)
30. This man is first in succession to the presidency (two words)
33. This was the prohibition amendment
34. The branch that makes laws
35. This Article deals with the states and the federal government
36. The amendment that deals with the rights of citizens, representation, and Civil War debts
37. The amendment that deals with the abolition of slavery
38. This Article deals with methods of amendment

Down

1. The President's advisers
2. The total number of Justices on the Supreme Court
3. Representatives are chosen every (how many) years
5. This Article deals with the legislative branch
6. Refers to the right of a court to hear and decide a case
7. This amendment is concerned with income tax
8. This amendment is concerned with the abolishment of the poll tax (two words)
10. Formal charges against an official of the federal government for misconduct in office or misuse of office
11. States the purpose of the Constitution
12. This amendment repealed the Eighteenth Amendment on Prohibition (two words)
13. The first ten amendments (three words)
16. This amendment deals with the limitation of the presidential term (two words)
17. Any kind of money a creditor is required by law to accept as payment of a debt (two words)
18. Free postal service for official mail (two words)
20. The number of years in the term of a president or vice-president
21. This Article deals with ratification of the Constitution
23. The Article that deals with the supreme law of the land
24. The refusal of the president to sign a bill passed by Congress
25. What represents the states in Congress
26. The branch that interprets laws
27. The amendment that deals with women's rights
28. The amendment that deals with presidential disability and succession (two words)
31. A Senator's term in years
32. The amendment that deals with the election of the president and the vice-president

Key

Across

1. Constitution
4. Supreme Court
9. bicameral
11. population
14. executive
15. two
19. three
20. Fifteenth
22. House of Representatives
29. separation of powers
30. vice-president
33. Eighteenth
34. legislative
35. four
36. Fourteenth
37. Thirteenth
38. five

Down

1. cabinet
2. nine
3. two
5. one
6. jurisdiction
7. Sixteenth
8. Twenty-fourth
10. impeachment
11. Preamble
12. Twenty-first
13. Bill of Rights
16. Twenty-second
17. legal tender
18. franking privilege
20. four
21. seven
23. six
24. veto
25. Senate
26. judicial
27. Nineteenth
28. Twenty-fifth
31. six
32. Twelfth

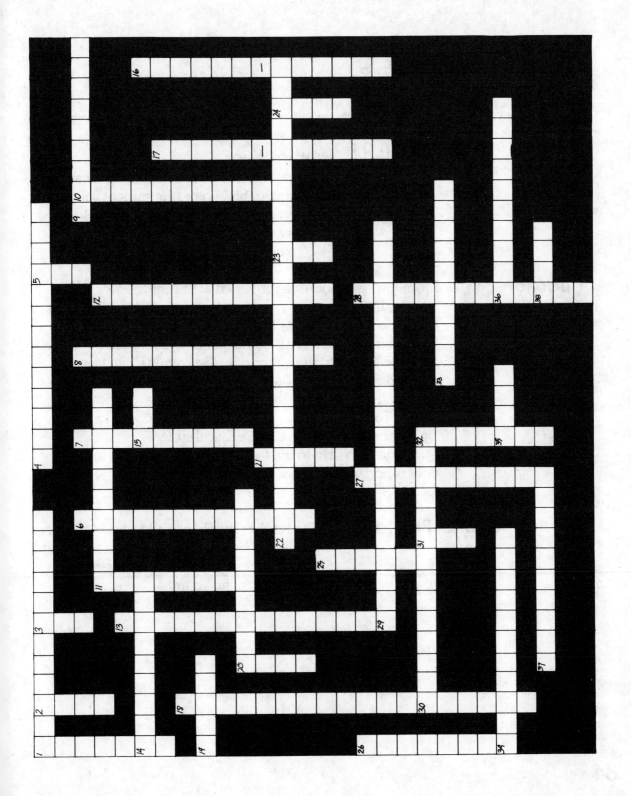

Center Activity:

Let's Find Out

Objective:
After completing the center and researching a country of his choice, the student will write a report on that country to be shared with the class at a later date.

Directions:

1. From the list of countries provided at the center, **select** the country that appeals to you and place your initials beside the country to indicate it has been chosen.
2. Using reference materials at the center and reference materials from the library, **write** a report on the country you have selected. The report should include the following points: geography, brief history of the country, primary products, ethnic groups, distinctive cultural traits or customs, kinds of agriculture and business, and political system.
3. Turn your report in to the teacher and be prepared to share your report with the class at a later time.

Materials Teacher Provides:

The teacher should provide a list of countries that would be appropriate for the report and several reference books and suggested references in the library.

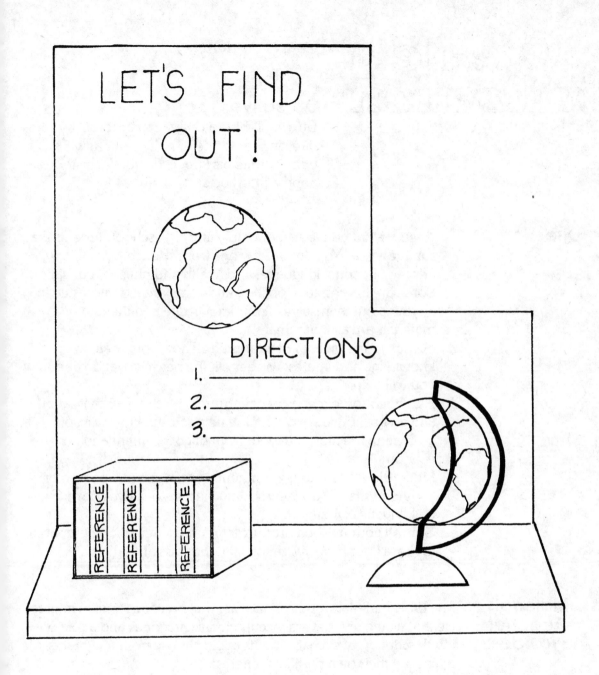

Create a Civilization

Objective:

By establishing a civilization according to the directions at the center, the student will demonstrate his knowledge of the historical approach to society.

Directions:

1. **Assume** that you are among only fifty high school students that survive a war. Your interests range from science to sociology, arts, engineering, language, and health and physical education. Some are interested in politics, and some are not interested in anything but themselves. Your knowledge and the raw materials are all that remain.

2. **Select** your own area of interest. **Tell** how your area of knowledge and interest will benefit the new civilization and how you will help.

3. **Establish** some means of government for the new civilization and an economic system for the new society. How will your civilization function with your form of government and economy?

4. Either **diagram** your governmental organizational pattern or **provide** a map of the new society in terms of a five-year plan for building the civilization.

5. **Submit** your finished product to your teacher and be prepared to share your new civilization with the class at a later date.

Materials Teacher Provides:

The basic materials for the center are the directions and an interest file that would give several occupational categories and a role or job description of each. Students could choose from the interest file or choose their own particular interest.

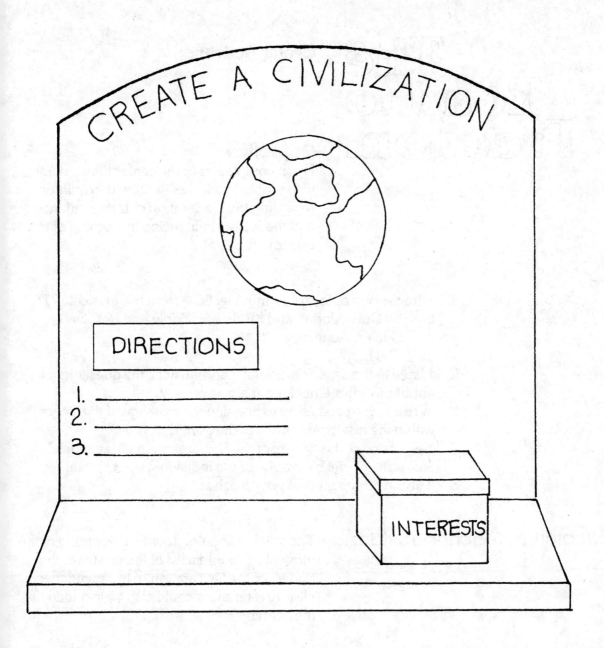

CREATE A CIVILIZATION

DIRECTIONS

1. _____
2. _____
3. _____

INTERESTS

The Road to Freedom

Center Activity:

Objective:
Upon completion of the center the student will be able to express the differing attitudes regarding the Declaration of Independence and the factors influencing the signing of the document.

Directions:

1. **Choose** one of the following selections from the musical *1776:*
   a. "Sit Down John" and "Riddle, Twiddle and Resolve"
   b. "But Mr. Adams"
   c. "The Egg"
2. **Listen** to the selection carefully and **answer** the questions about the lyrics. **Check** your answers.
3. **Write** a one-page essay expressing the message of the singer within the historical context of the period.
4. **Select** one of the signers of the Declaration of Independence and **write** a brief biography of the individual you choose.
5. **Turn in** both papers to your teacher.

Materials Teacher Provides:

The teacher should provide a recording of the musical *1776* and a list of the names of the signers of the Declaration of Independence. History references could also be included at the center.

THE ROAD TO FREEDOM

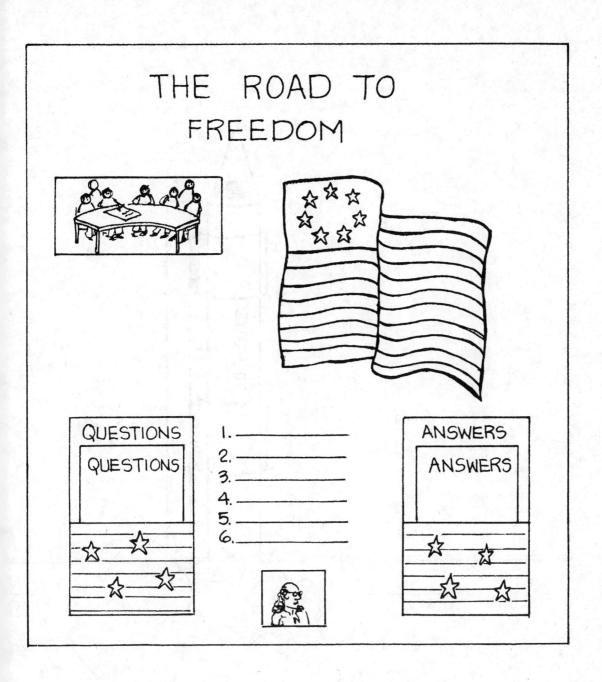

QUESTIONS

QUESTIONS

1. _____
2. _____
3. _____
4. _____
5. _____
6. _____

ANSWERS

ANSWERS

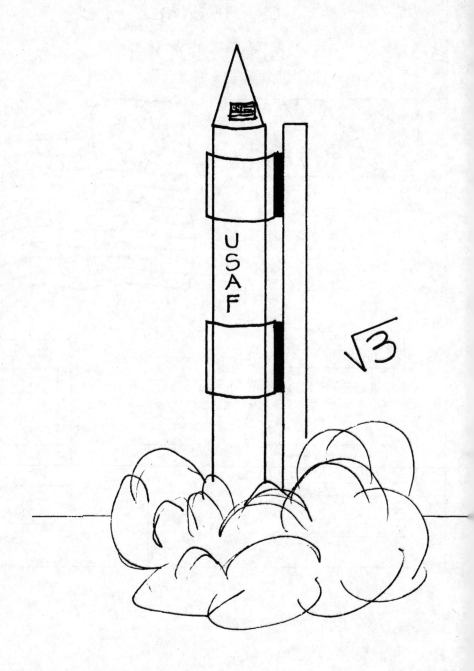

Science and Math

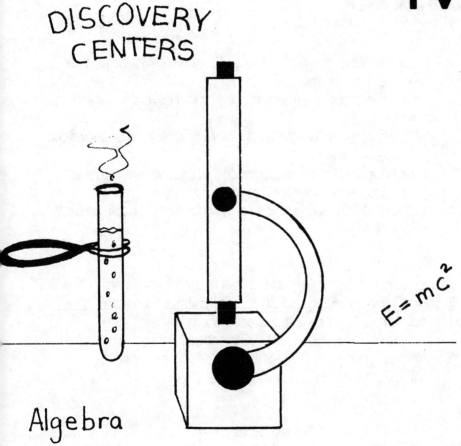

DISCOVERY CENTERS

$E = mc^2$

Algebra

Unit: Plant and Animal Cells

Concept:
The cell is the basic building block of living organisms both in plants and animals. The cell has many parts, and plant and animal cells differ in their composition.

Objectives:

After completing the unit on plant and animal cells, the student should be able to

1. name the basic parts of the cell and give the function of each
2. differentiate between plant and animal cells and state how they differ
3. sketch both plant and animal cells as viewed in the microscope and label the major parts
4. define the terms associated with the unit on plant and animal cells

Unit Requirements:

Students must complete all of the learning centers in the unit. Evaluation will be based on the following criteria:

1. Plant and Animal Cells Center: 25 percent
2. Put the Bite on the Facts: 20 percent
3. What Can You Tell About a Cell?: 25 percent
4. Unit Examination: 30 percent

Time: Seven class periods.

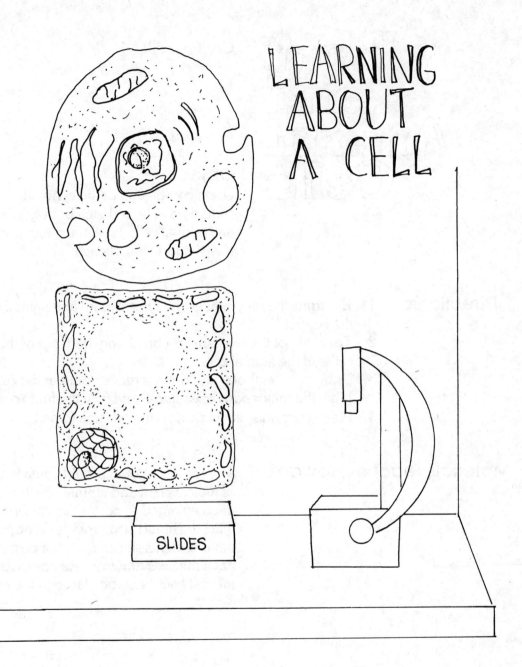

LEARNING ABOUT A CELL

SLIDES

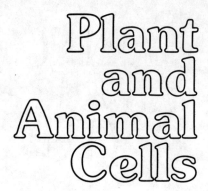

Plant and Animal Cells

Center 1:

Objective:

Upon completion of the center the student should be able to sketch both typical plant and animal cells, label the major parts, and give the function of each.

Directions:

1. **Examine** the diagrams of the typical plant and animal cells at the center.
2. **Take** one of the worksheets containing drawings of the plant cell and the animal cell.
3. Using your textbook and the reference books at the center, **label** the major parts of each cell and give the functions of each.
4. **Place** your finished worksheet in your unit folder.

Materials Teacher Provides:

The teacher should provide detailed drawings of typical plant and animal cells that have been enlarged to poster dimensions. The teacher should also provide worksheets (or have students sketch from the poster) that have the cells drawn in. Reference books on the cell could also be placed at the center.

PLANT AND ANIMAL CELLS

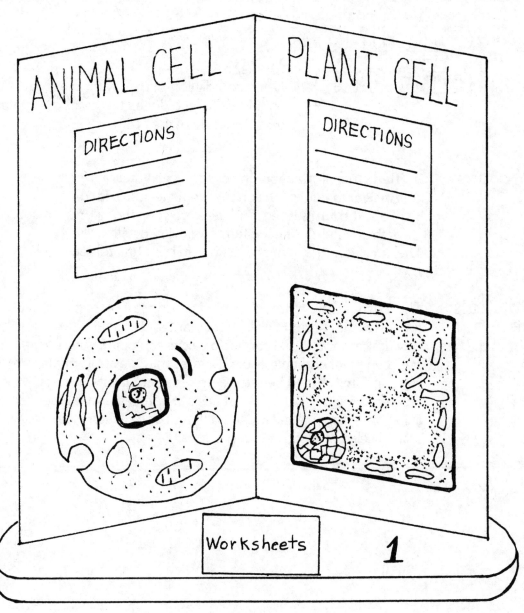

ANIMAL CELL

DIRECTIONS

PLANT CELL

DIRECTIONS

Worksheets

1

Put the Bite on the Facts

Objective:
Upon completion of the center the student should be able to define the terms associated with the study of the cell.

Directions:

1. **Read** the information on cells and cell functions.
2. **Answer** the questions on the worksheet provided.
3. **Copy** the terms listed, and using your textbook or the resources at the center **define** the terms associated with cells.
4. **Place** your questions and terms in your unit folder.

Materials Teacher Provides:

The teacher should provide a brief description of the basic life processes that occur in cells, both plant and animal. The description should also contain a discussion of the differences between plant and animal cells. Terms that are appropriate to the class and unit should be listed at the center. Questions to be answered might include: What basic life processes are essential for living organisms? What are the differences between plant and animal cells? How do cells reproduce?

PUT THE BITE ON THE FACTS

KNOWING ABOUT CELLS

2

DIRECTIONS	TERMS
1. READ _____ _____	nucleus
	osmosis
2. ANSWER _____ _____	respiration
	organelle
	digestion
3. DEFINE _____ _____	diffusion
	organism
	ingestion

What Can You Tell About a Cell?

Center 3:

Objective:

The student will be able to locate both plant and animal cells on prepared slides and will sketch the cells and label the major parts visible in the microscope.

Directions:

1. **Take** a microscope from the microscope case.
2. **Pick up** the prepared slides of plant and animal cells.
3. After getting each cell in focus under the microscope, **identify** the major parts of the cell that are visible.
4. **Sketch** each cell and label the parts that are visible under the microscope.
5. **Place** your finished sketches in your unit folder.

Materials Teacher Provides:

The teacher should provide the microscopes and the prepared slides of plant and animal cells. To make the lab more elaborate, students could prepare their own slides by scraping cells from the inside of their mouth and examining cells of *Elodea*.

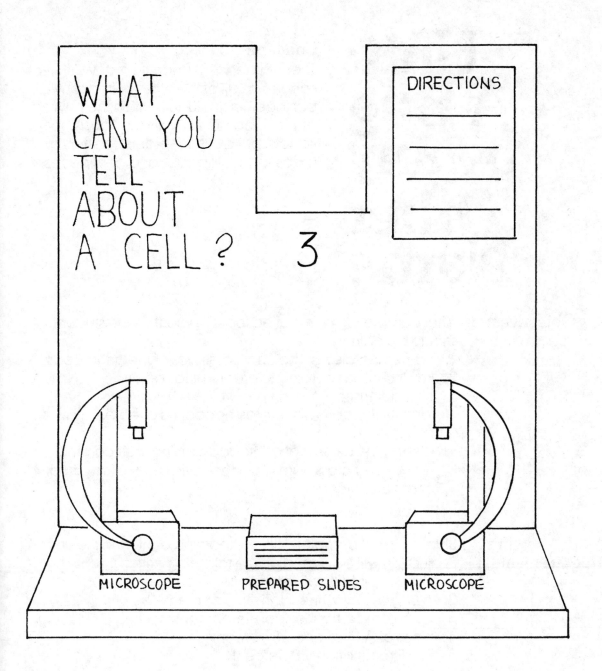

WHAT CAN YOU TELL ABOUT A CELL? 3

DIRECTIONS

MICROSCOPE   PREPARED SLIDES   MICROSCOPE

Unit: A Bug by any Other Name

Concept:
The arthropods include as many different species as all of the other animal phyla put together. Included within the phylum Arthropoda are not only the "bugs," or insects, but also the spiders, lobsters and crabs, and millipedes and centipedes.

Objectives:
After completing all required learning centers the student should be able to
1. name and discuss the characteristics of the arthropods
2. key insects according to order, using specific characteristics
3. identify the parts of the grasshopper as a representative insect
4. identify the classes of arthropods, giving their common name, their class name, and specific body or structural characteristics

Unit Requirements:
Students must complete all four learning centers in the unit. Evaluation will be based on the following criteria:
1. Finding Out About Arthropods: 15 percent
2. A Bug by Any Other Name: 15 percent
3. Parts of the Grasshopper: 25 percent
4. Kinds of Arthropods: 25 percent
5. Unit Examination: 20 percent

Time: Twelve class periods.

100

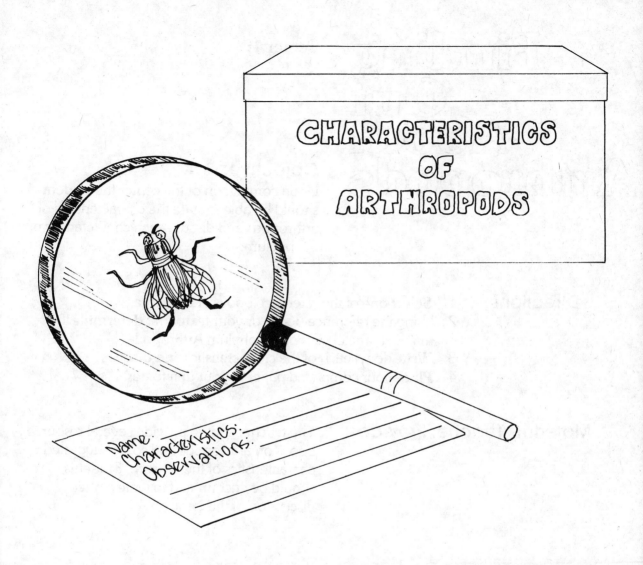

CHARACTERISTICS
OF
ARTHROPODS

Name:
Characteristics:
Observations:

Finding Out About Arthropods

Objective:

Upon completion of the center the student should be able to state the characteristics of arthropods and discuss each characteristic of the phylum.

Directions:

1. **Select** one of the reference books at the center.
2. Using the reference books or your textbook, **determine** the major characteristics of the phylum Arthropoda.
3. **Write** down each of the characteristics and **discuss** it.
4. **Place** your completed paper in your unit folder.

Materials Teacher Provides:

The teacher should provide several resource books on arthropods and some suggested characteristics of the phylum. Students should be encouraged to write a brief discussion of this large phylum.

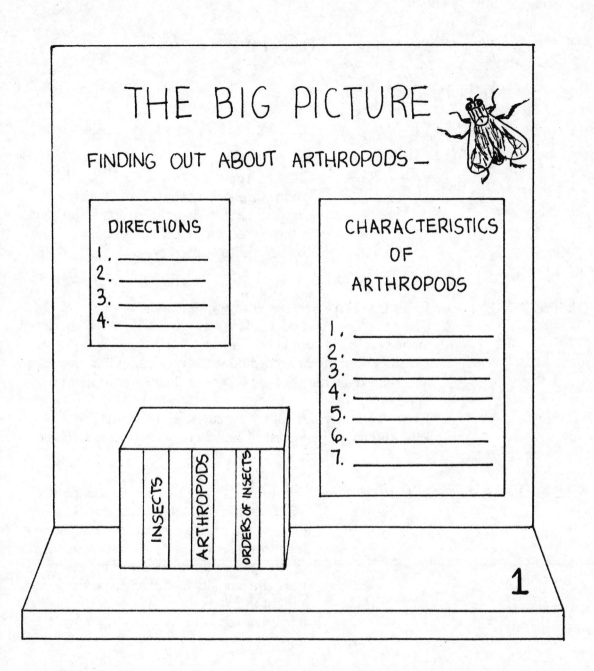

THE BIG PICTURE

FINDING OUT ABOUT ARTHROPODS —

DIRECTIONS

1. _____
2. _____
3. _____
4. _____

CHARACTERISTICS OF ARTHROPODS

1. _____
2. _____
3. _____
4. _____
5. _____
6. _____
7. _____

INSECTS   ARTHROPODS   ORDERS OF INSECTS

1

A Bug by any Other Name

Center 2:

Objective:
Upon completion of the center the student should be able to key the insects at the center to the correct order, using the specific characteristics of each order.

Directions:
1. **Examine** each insect specimen pinned in the box.
2. Using the "Keying Orders of Insects" sheet, **key** each specimen in the box to the correct order.
3. **Number** your paper according to the number of the specimen and **record** the name of the order beside the appropriate number.
4. **Check** your answers with the answers at the center.
5. **Place** your completed list of keyed insects in your unit folder.

Materials Teacher Provides:
The teacher should provide a set of pinned insects for the students to examine. The teacher should also provide several resource books for keying insects to their correct order, using specific criteria. To make the center more challenging, the teacher could ask each student to collect three to five specimens from different insect orders.

"A BUG BY ANY OTHER NAME"

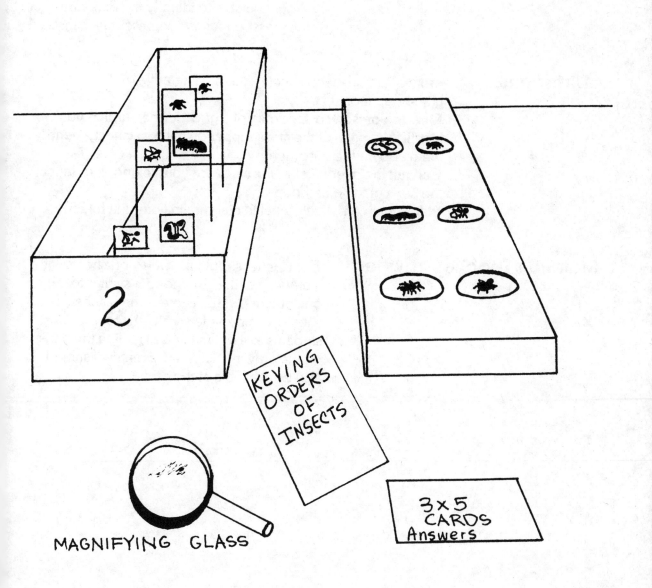

Center 3:

Parts of the Grasshopper

Objective:

After completing the center the student should be able to identify the major parts of the grasshopper as a representative insect.

Directions:

1. **Take** one of the worksheets with the diagram of the grasshopper on it.
2. **Obtain** a preserved specimen of a grasshopper, and as you identify the parts of the grasshopper on the worksheet, **identify** them also on the specimen.
3. **Consult** the references at the center or your textbook to **label** the parts of the grasshopper.
4. **Place** your completely labeled diagram in your unit folder.

Materials Teacher Provides:

The teacher should provide worksheets with a drawing of the grasshopper similar to the one outlined at the center. The teacher should also provide specimens for the students to examine while labeling the parts on the drawing. Reference material should also be available at the center.

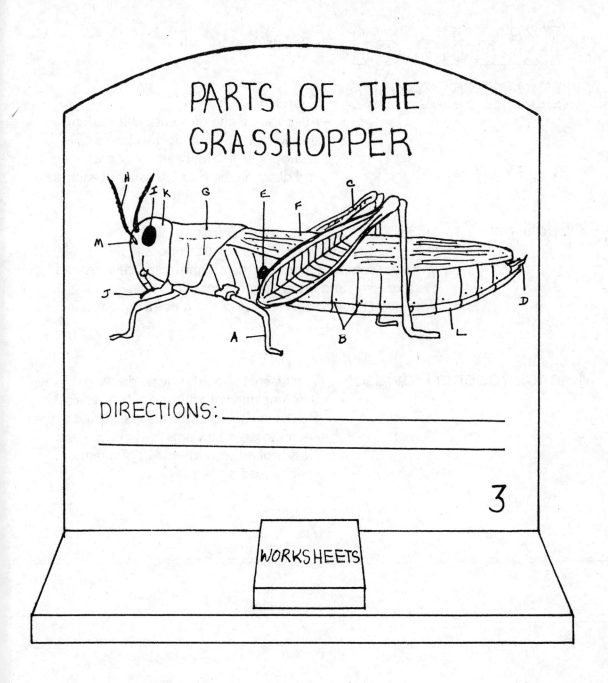

PARTS OF THE GRASSHOPPER

DIRECTIONS: _____

_____

3

WORKSHEETS

Kinds of Arthropods

Objective:

After completing the center the student should be able to name the classes of arthropods, give an example of each class, and describe the characteristics of each class.

Directions:

1. On a sheet of paper, **number** from one to five.
2. Using the drawings of the kinds of arthropods at the center, **write** the common name for the organism, the class name for the organism, and the characteristics of the class.
3. When you have completed the chart, **place** it in your unit folder.

Materials Teacher Provides:

The teacher should provide drawings of the different kinds of arthropods (poster size). Reference books could also be placed at the center to assist students in identifying the classes of arthropods and in giving the characteristics of each class.

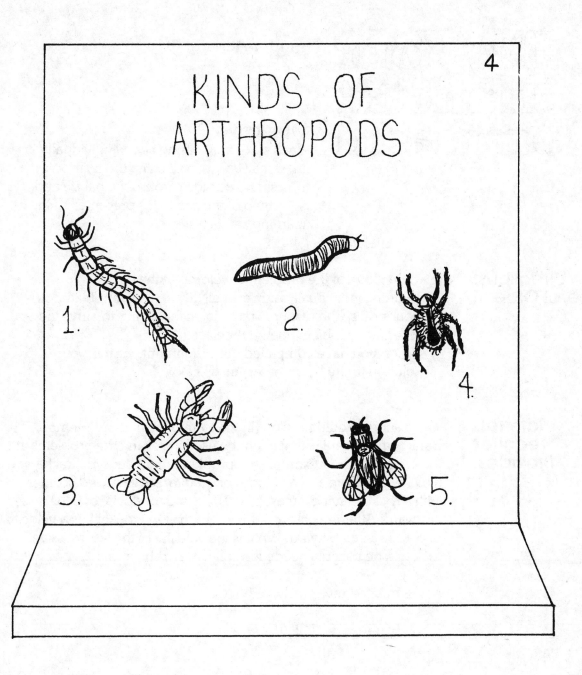

KINDS OF
ARTHROPODS

4

1.

2.

3.

4.

5.

109

Try Your Hand at Command

Objective:

Each student, working either individually or in a small group, will, using the textbook, notes, and outside resources, analyze and solve two of the problems presented at the learning center.

Directions:
(General Orders)

1. **Select** one of the problem envelopes at the center.
2. Working individually or in a small group, use your textbook, your notes, and resource material at the center to **solve** the kinematic problem you have selected.
3. When you have completed the assignment, **turn in** your solution to the "Computer Answer Box."

Materials
Teacher
Provides:

The teacher should provide (in the form of a chart or "Memory Bank") the formulas that might be used in solving the problems in the envelopes. For example the problem might be: A rocket having a mass of 0.25 kg and a velocity of 0.20 m/sec eastward collides with a rocket having a mass of 0.10 kg and a velocity of 0.10 m/sec eastward. After the collision, the more massive rocket has a velocity of 0.15 m/sec eastward. What is the velocity of the less massive rocket? The formula needed to solve the problem is:

$$mv_i + m'v_i' = mv_f + m'v_f'$$

$$v_f' = \frac{mv_i + m'v_i' - mv_f}{m'}$$

Answer: $(v_f') = 0.22$ m/sec eastward

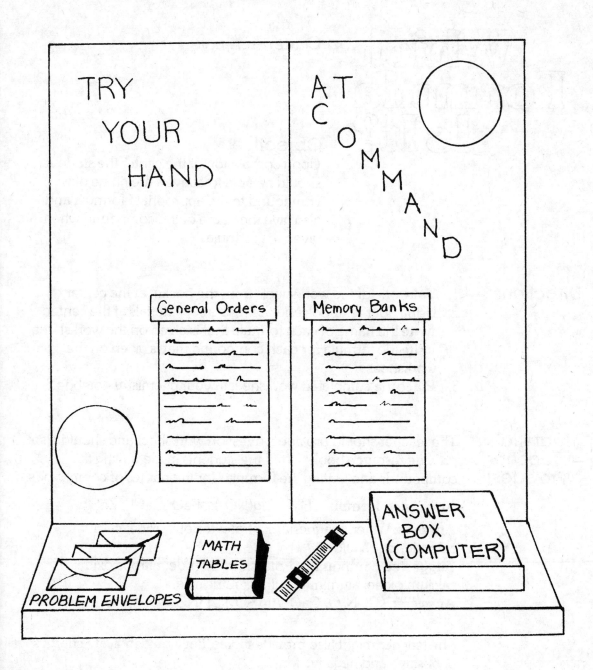

Which Formula Is It?

Center Activity:

Objective:
Upon completion of the center the student should be able to convert the name of a compound to the appropriate formula and also give the name of the compound when given the formula.

Directions:
1. **Take** one of the worksheets from the pocket at the center.
2. Using your textbook and the resource materials at the center, **write** the name of each formula that is given on the worksheet; **write** the formula for each compound that is given on the worksheet.
3. **Place** the completed worksheet in your chemistry notebook.

Materials Teacher Provides:
The teacher should provide a question worksheet and should also provide resource books to aid the students in identifying the compounds and writing the formulas for the names of compounds.

Suggested formulas: H_2O; $Mg(NO_3)_2$; FeO; $CaCl_2$; ZnS

Answers: Water; magnesium nitrate; ferrous oxide; calcium chloride; zinc sulfide.

Suggested compounds: Potassium chloride; nitrous oxide; calcium oxide; aluminum sulfate; nitric acid.

Answers: KCl, N_2O, CaO, $Al_2(SO_4)_3$, HNO_3

The teacher might also provide tables that would indicate charges of positive and negative ions.

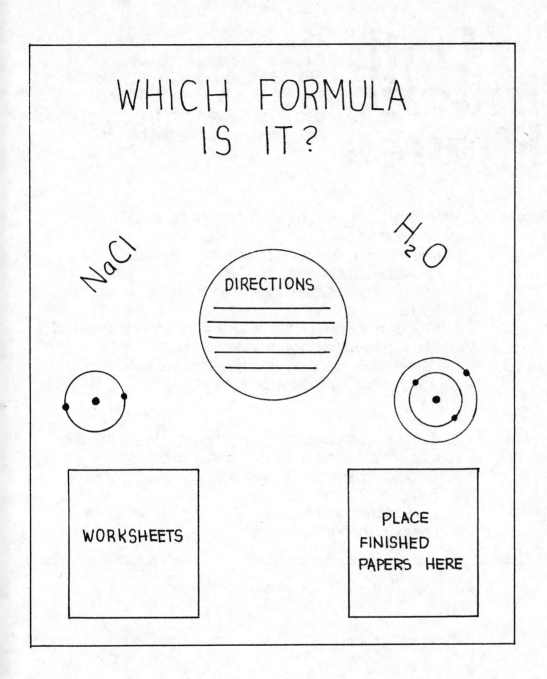

WHICH FORMULA
IS IT?

NaCl

H_2O

DIRECTIONS

WORKSHEETS

PLACE
FINISHED
PAPERS HERE

Unit: Geometric Figures

Concept:
Geometric figures have special properties, qualities, and names. Students should become familiar with the kinds of geometric figures and the mathematical properties associated with them.

Objectives:
After completing the unit on geometric figures, the student should be able to
1. name seven geometric shapes and give the characteristics of each
2. define the terms associated with the study of geometric figures
3. define "polygon" and give examples and characteristics found in specific polygons
4. define "quadrilateral" and give the characteristics and names of at least four examples

Unit Requirements:
All students must complete all learning centers in the unit. Evaluation will be based on the following criteria:
1. Geometric Shapes: 20 percent
2. Polygons: 20 percent
3. Quadrilaterals: 25 percent
4. Unit Examination: 35 percent

Time: Ten class periods.

114

Geometric Shapes

Center 1:

Objective:
Upon completion of the center the student should be able to define the terms associated with the study of geometric shapes.

Directions:
1. **View** the filmstrip that discusses terms associated with geometric shapes.
2. **Copy** the terms from the center onto a sheet of paper, and using your textbook and the information from the filmstrip, **define** the terms.
3. **Place** your completed definitions in your unit folder.

Materials Teacher Provides:

The teacher should provide a filmstrip that discusses geometric shapes ("Introducing Shapes, Lines and Angles," CORF, 1966, color) or a set of overhead transparencies presenting terms associated with geometric shapes. Terms for the center include: parallel, perpendicular, angle, line segment, polygon, quadrilateral, transversal line, corresponding angles, congruent.

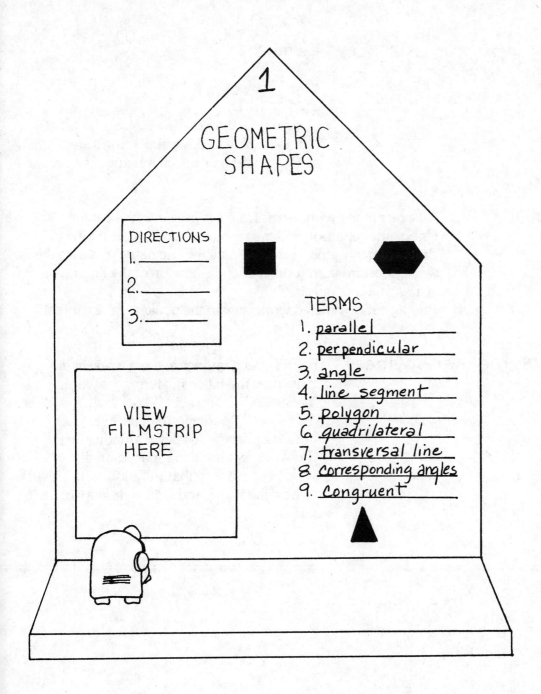

1

GEOMETRIC SHAPES

DIRECTIONS
1. _____
2. _____
3. _____

VIEW
FILMSTRIP
HERE

TERMS
1. parallel _____
2. perpendicular _____
3. angle _____
4. line segment _____
5. polygon _____
6. quadrilateral _____
7. transversal line _____
8. corresponding angles _____
9. congruent _____

Polygons

Center 2:

Objective:

Upon completion of the center the student should be able to draw and name seven polygons and give the characteristics of each.

Directions:

1. **Take** one of the worksheets from the pocket at the center.
2. Using your textbook and the resource books at the center, **draw** the geometric figure that matches the name given on the worksheet and then **write** a brief description of the figure, giving its characteristics.
3. **Place** your completed worksheet in the pocket at the center.

Materials Teacher Provides:

The teacher should prepare a worksheet containing the following terms: "square," "rectangle," "trapezoid," "octagon," "hexagon," "pentagon," "triangle" (equilateral and isosceles), "quadrilateral." These names should be spaced on the worksheet in a way that will allow the student to draw the figure and write a description of it.

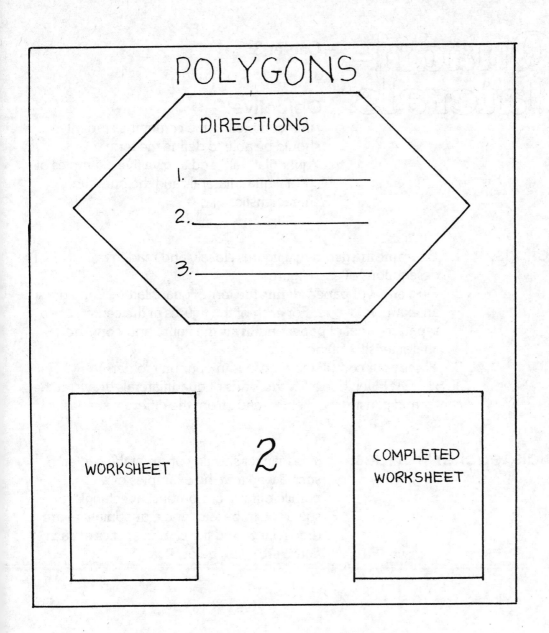

POLYGONS

DIRECTIONS

1. _____

2. _____

3. _____

WORKSHEET

2

COMPLETED
WORKSHEET

119

Quadri-laterals

Center 3:

Objective:

After completing the center the student should be able to define the term "quadrilateral" and to give five examples of special quadrilaterals and their unique characteristics.

Directions:

1. **Examine** the geometric figures closely and read the descriptions of each figure.
2. On a sheet of paper, **define** the term "quadrilateral" and draw an example of one. For each of the figures at the center, use a separate sheet of paper and **draw** the figure and **copy** the characteristics of the figure.
3. **Place** your completed drawings in your unit folder.

JUST FOR FUN: Use all of the kinds of quadrilaterals drawn at the center and construct a picture made from the different shapes.

Materials Teacher Provides:

The teacher should construct the center in such a way that the examples of a parallelogram, a rhombus, a rectangle, a square, a trapezoid, and a quadrilateral are drawn large and the characteristics of each figure are given below it.

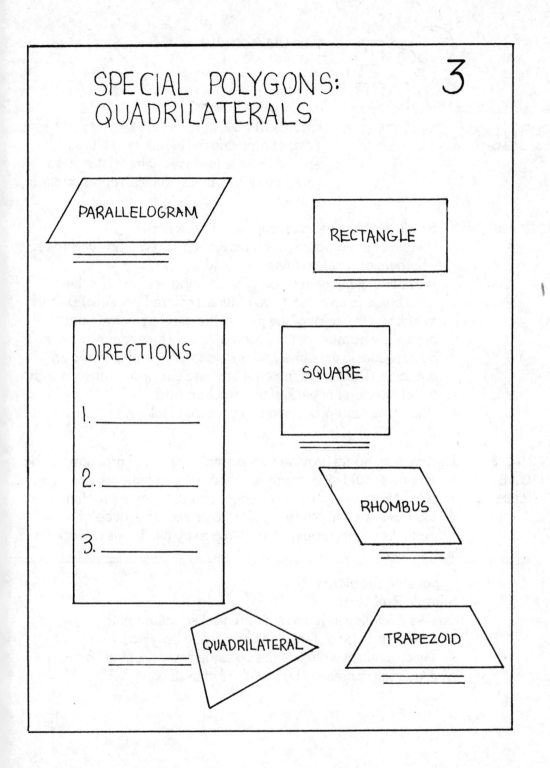

SPECIAL POLYGONS:
QUADRILATERALS

3

PARALLELOGRAM

RECTANGLE

DIRECTIONS

SQUARE

1. _____

2. _____

3. _____

RHOMBUS

QUADRILATERAL

TRAPEZOID

Can You Translate?

Objective:

After completing the center the student should be able to correctly translate stated problems into a mathematical representation.

Directions:

1. **Study** the translation examples at the center.
2. Do two of the practice problems and check your answers to see whether you worked them correctly.
3. **Work** five of the word problems from the pockets. (Problems must come from at least two different colored pockets.) Be sure to indicate the color of the pocket the problem came from beside the number of the problem. **Solve** the word problems by introducing variables and translating the problem into an equation. Then solve the equation and check your answer with the answer on the back of the problem card.
4. **Place** your completed work in your math folder.

Materials Teacher Provides:

The teacher should provide two examples of stated problems at the center and should give examples of how the statements are translated into an equation and then solved. Sample problems should be divided into three groups to provide the levels of difficulty. Students should be required to try two levels in working five problems.

Suggested Problems:
Sample Problems
Express the following as a mathematical equation:
1. One-fourth the distance between two cities ($\frac{1}{4}d$)
2. Twice a number diminished by some other number ($2x - y$)
3. A quantity increased by one-third of itself ($x + \frac{1}{3}x$)

Level I Problem

Some people consider 2 and ¾ times their annual income a fair investment in a home. If the Jones family followed this rule and bought a home for $28,600, what is their annual income?

Answer: $2\frac{3}{4}a = \$28,600$

$\qquad a = (28,600)(4/11)$

$\qquad a = \$10,400$

Level II Problem

I am thinking of a number such that four times the number diminished by seven is fifty-three. What is the number?

Answer: $4n - 7 = 53$

$\qquad 4n = 60$

$\qquad n = 15$

Level III Problem

Mary's height is 3 and ½ inches less than Susan's height. If Susan is 63 and ¼ inches tall, how tall is Mary?

Answer: $3\frac{1}{2}x = 63\frac{1}{4}$

$\qquad x = 253/4 - 14/4$

$\qquad x = 59\frac{3}{4}$ inches

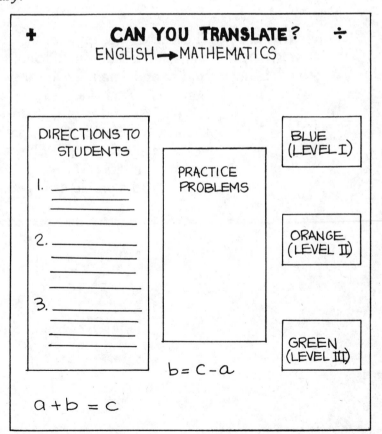

Math Bingo

Objective:

Upon completion of the center the student should be able to work a given set of problems correctly.

Directions:

1. **Select** a "Bingo" card at the center. (The center is designed for a maximum of seven players.)
2. When everyone is ready, **draw** a problem card from the deck. **Work** the indicated problem, and if you have the answer on your bingo card, **cover** the answer with a token.
3. The first one to work the problems and complete a line vertically, horizontally, or diagonally wins.

Materials Teacher Provides:

The teacher must provide the "Bingo" game. In setting up the game, the teacher should take several problems from the unit studied and determine the answers. Using the answers as the numbers for the bingo cards (problem answers could be coded B-44, I-768, and so on), the teacher should make seven cards with the answers to at least thirty problems in the pool of numbers. In designing the cards, a FREE space could be given at each corner and in the middle. The teacher should also provide the problem deck, with the problems stated on the front and the answers on the back.

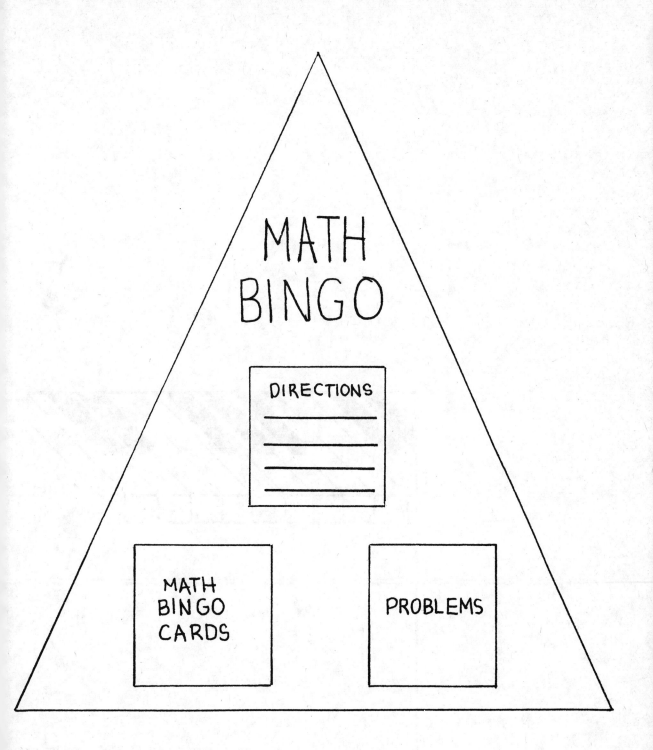

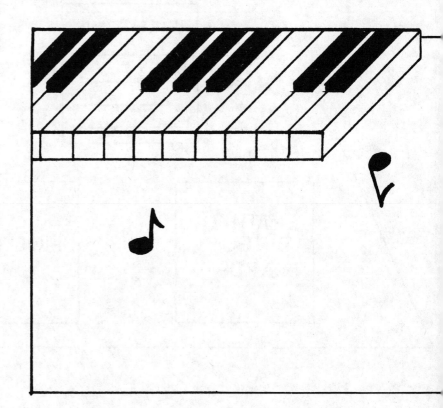

Art
and
Music

Unit: Watercolor

Concept:
Watercolor is an effective art medium that students need to explore in the process of developing art concepts and creative expression.

Objectives:
Upon completion of the assigned learning centers the student should be able to
1. demonstrate the effect of watercolor on a wet surface and discuss the importance of water as the controlling medium in watercolor painting
2. demonstrate an ability to use watercolor effectively by completing three watercolor projects
3. state how watercolor reacts as a medium
4. use color and the watercolor medium to express a feeling such as anger, happiness, or sadness

Unit Requirements:
All students must complete each center in the watercolor unit. Evaluation will be based on the following criteria:
1. Basic Watercolor Steps: 40 percent
2. Wet Watercolor: 30 percent
3. Mood Paintings: 30 percent

Time: Fifteen class periods.

EXPERIMENT!

What happens with different
amounts of water or paint?

Basic Watercolor Steps

Center 1:

Objective:
After completing the center the student should be able to demonstrate the ability to use watercolor effectively as an artistic medium by completing three projects. The student should also be able to state the characteristics of watercolor as a medium.

Directions: (do these steps in sequence)

1. *Flatwash.* **Take** two sheets of watercolor paper, one large brush, a tube of watercolor (any color), a can of water, an easel, and an instruction sheet for doing a flatwash. Use your first sheet of watercolor paper to become proficient in the use of the watercolor medium. Use the second sheet to paint on and **submit** your finished work to the teacher for evaluation.
2. *Graded wash.* **Take** two sheets of watercolor paper, the same equipment as in Step 1, and the instructions for doing a graded wash. **Practice** on your first sheet and use the second sheet to **submit** as your finished project.
3. *Dry Brush.* Again, take two sheets of watercolor paper and the directions for dry brush. **Practice** on your first sheet and **turn in** your second product.

Materials Teacher Provides:
The teacher should supply all the necessary materials for the unit, such as easels, tubes of watercolor paint, brushes, and watercolor paper. The teacher should also provide the directions for doing a flatwash, a graded wash, and a dry brush painting.

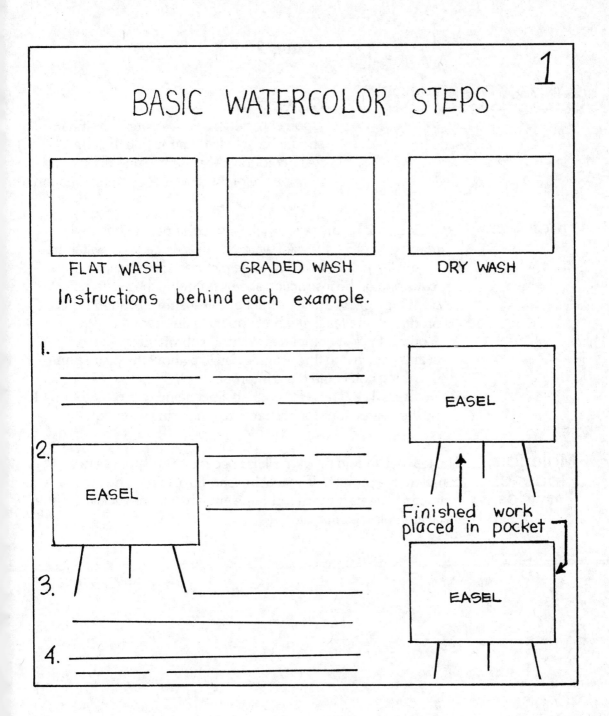

BASIC WATERCOLOR STEPS

1

FLAT WASH   GRADED WASH   DRY WASH

Instructions behind each example.

1. _____

2. EASEL

EASEL

Finished work
placed in pocket

3. _____

EASEL

4. _____

131

Wet Watercolor

Center 2:

Objective:
Upon completion of the center the student should be able to demonstrate the effect of watercolor on a wet surface and discuss the importance of water as a controlling medium.

Directions:

1. **Pick up** your materials: easel, watercolor paper stretched on frames, brushes, tubes of watercolor paint, cans for water, tray for mixing paints, and magazine pictures of landscapes.
2. **Take** one of the instruction sheets for doing the landscape painting. Follow those instructions and **submit** your finished product to the teacher when you have finished.
3. Along with your completed picture, **submit** your own evaluation, giving three points you like about the picture and one thing you could do to improve it.
4. Do Steps 1, 2, and 3 for your abstract painting project, but **pick up** the instructions for abstract painting using watercolor.

Materials Teacher Provides:

The teacher should provide all the necessary art supplies needed to complete the projects. The teacher should also provide the instruction sheets for the landscape and abstract projects using the wet watercolor technique.

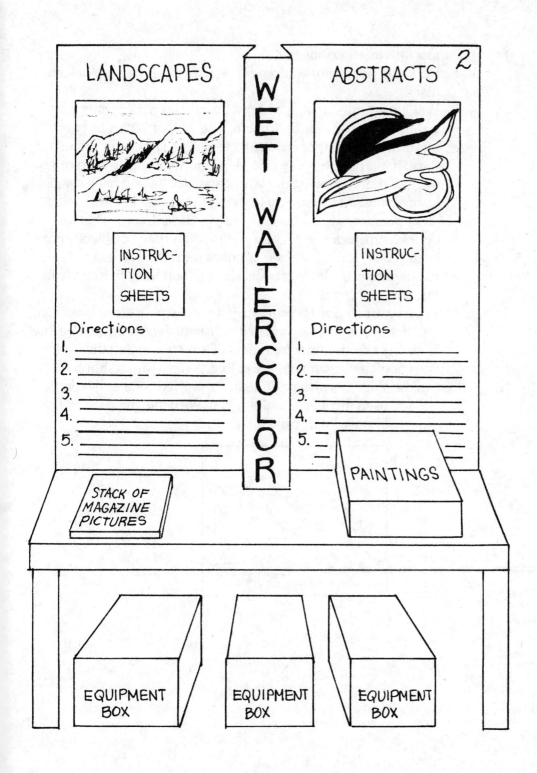

LANDSCAPES

WET WATERCOLOR

ABSTRACTS

2

INSTRUCTION SHEETS

Directions
1. _____
2. _____
3. _____
4. _____
5. _____

INSTRUCTION SHEETS

Directions
1. _____
2. _____
3. _____
4. _____
5. _____

STACK OF MAGAZINE PICTURES

PAINTINGS

EQUIPMENT BOX

EQUIPMENT BOX

EQUIPMENT BOX

Landscape Instructions

1. Set up all necessary equipment. Mix three primary colors and black.
2. With your large brush, paint the watercolor paper with clear water, wetting the entire surface. Use a lot of water, but avoid puddles on the paper (you can blot with a sponge or paper towel if this happens). Quickly fill your brush with the color you want and start copying the landscape picture you have selected from a magazine (don't try to get all the details in). This will be an impressionistic landscape—fuzzy, like a dream. Think of your picture as areas of color, rather than specific objects. Paint in all colors, filling the page. Paint as much as you can before the paper dries. When it begins to dry, you have finished with this part of the picture.
3. When your picture is completely dry, take your small brush and add details, as you learned in the dry brush technique. Use fine lines and sketch rather than draw. Don't worry that the sketch lines don't exactly match the colored areas—they shouldn't.

Comment: With this picture you started with a scene and have used the wet technique to make it into an impressionistic painting.

Abstract Painting Instructions

1. Set up all necessary equipment. Mix three primary paints with water. Have a can of water for cleaning brushes and one with clear water.

2. With your large brush, paint the paper with clear water, wetting the whole surface. Use a lot of water but avoid puddles (you can blot with a sponge or paper towel if this happens). Quickly fill the brush with color and touch to paper. An explosion of color will radiate out. Put this color on various places on the paper as you like. Now add a second color (with a clean brush) and touch the paper again to get another explosion of color radiating out (if two colors meet, a secondary color will appear). Try a third color on the paper, but leave some white paper showing. If you like, you can pick up the canvas and turn it to let the colors run together even more. Let the painting dry.

3. With a fine black felt-tipped pen draw in lines to make a design or scene. Do this after studying the painting to determine the different images in it. Add some details and study the whole effect of the painting before adding more.

Comment: With this picture you started with a nonobjective painting and made it into a scene or design by adding details that the colors suggested to you.

Mood Paintings

Objective:

After completing the center the student should be able to express a feeling using colors and the watercolor medium.

Directions:

1. *Mood Portrait.* Think about color and what mood you associate with colors. When you are sad we say you are "blue"; when you are happy, we say you're just "rosie"; when you are envious we say you're "green with envy"; if things look "black," they are pretty hopeless. Take a long look in the mirror. Face: round, square, oval, long? Hair: curly, long, short, straight? Ears: big, little, close to head? Eyes: big, little, closed partly, wide open? Mouth: small, large, narrow, wide, turned up? **Sketch** yourself using pencil and then draw in the face using waterproof ink. Think of all the different ways you felt this week. **Paint** most of the face with the color that represents the mood you've had most of the week, then use other colors in the amounts that show how you have felt during the week. On the back of the portrait **write** a brief summary of your week, explaining the significance of the colors. **Place** the portrait in your unit folder.

2. *Mood Pictures Painted to Music.* Go to one of the easels and get art equipment ready. **Take** a cassette tape player and turn on the music. **Listen** for a few minutes to get the mood of the music, then take paint on your brush that has the color that represents the mood of the music to you. Use a wet or dry canvas, whole bursts of colors or lines—**paint** whatever the music feels like to you. Place your name on the back of the picture and **write** a brief description of the mood the music created and how it is represented in the picture. **Place** the finished picture in your unit folder.

3. *Other Mood Pictures.* **Pick** one of the following topics to paint: the (saddest, angriest, happiest, loneliest) person I know; the angry sea; the threatening storm; the gaiety of a (circus, carnival, Mardi gras), the excitement of a (ball game, stock car race, horse race). **Sketch** your scene first and then use waterproof black ink to go over your sketch. **Apply** the colors that represent the scene and mood you have selected. **Write** a few lines about your picture on the back and sign it. **Place** the completed picture in your unit folder.

Materials Teacher Provides:

The teacher should provide all of the necessary art supplies. The teacher should also provide a mirror for the mood portrait activity, a cassette tape recorder and music tapes for the mood created by music, and perhaps examples of art that reflect different moods for the students to examine.

MOOD PAINTINGS   3

(EVERYONE DOES #1 CENTER & THEN YOU MAY DO EITHER
ONE OF THE OTHERS OR BOTH IF YOU LIKE)

#I MOOD   PORTRAITS

DIRECTIONS

POCKET   FOR
MOOD   PORTRAITS

1. _____
2. _____
3. _____
4. _____

MIRRORS   5. _____

#II MUSIC MOOD PICTURES

RECORD POCKET

1. _____
2. _____
3. _____

CASSETTE
PLAYER
&
TAPES

FOR MUSIC MOOD
PICTURES

#III OTHER MOOD PICTURES

1. _____   4. _____
2. _____   5. _____
3. _____   6. _____

POCKET FOR
MOOD PICTURES

Get the Whole Idea

Center Activity:

Objective:

Upon completing the center activity the student will be able to construct a design composition with free methods to explore the possibilities of color and shape and will consider arrangement and composition in the judgment of an art piece.

Directions:

1. Without looking, **reach into** the cut-out hole and take out four objects.
2. Using any color or combination of colors, **pour** a small amount of tempera paint into the tray provided.
3. Using your objects as tools for painting or printing, **create** a design on the paper provided. You may use each object to create a unique design on four sheets of paper, or you may combine the objects into the creation of one design.
4. On the back of your design(s) **answer** the following questions: How does the effect of each object contribute to the composition? How does the choice of color contribute to the composition? Is there repetition? Contrast? Is there a distinguishable design or subject matter?
5. **Place** your completed composition in your art folder.

Materials Teacher Provides:

The teacher should provide the objects in the cut-out hole of the center. Objects could include bottle caps, Q-tips, rubber bands, straws, small pieces of sponge, small pebbles, or paper clips. The teacher should also provide the primary colors of tempera paint and the trays to mix the paint in, along with art paper on which to create the design.

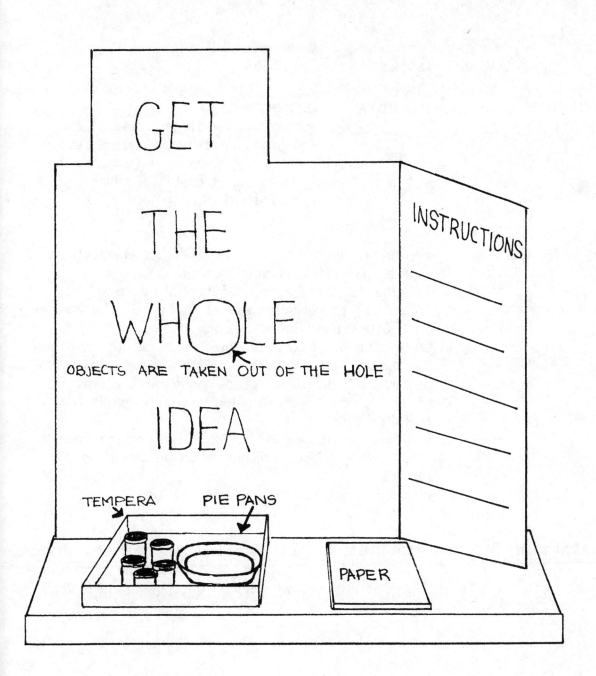

Contour Line

Objective:

After completing the center the student should be able to "see" objects in view of light, color, shape, line, and form and should be able to define contour line, having experimented with a contour-line drawing.

Directions:

1. **Flip** through the magazine pictures at the center and **choose** a desirable picture for a contour drawing.
2. **Tack** the picture to the cardboard behind the drawing box.
3. **Take** a sheet of drawing paper and place it inside the drawing box. Put both hands inside the box.
4. **Observe** the magazine picture before you. Let your eyes roam over the contour and let your hand inside the box **draw** what your eye sees. Be sure to use one continuous line.
5. After completing the drawing, **look** at your composition. Does it look like the picture?
6. **Evaluate** your drawing in terms of line, weight, and space relationships. Make your comments on the back of the composition.
7. **Place** your completed work in your art folder.

Materials Teacher Provides:

The teacher should provide several magazine pictures that would be suitable for contour drawing and the drawing box and paper.

CONTOUR DRAWING

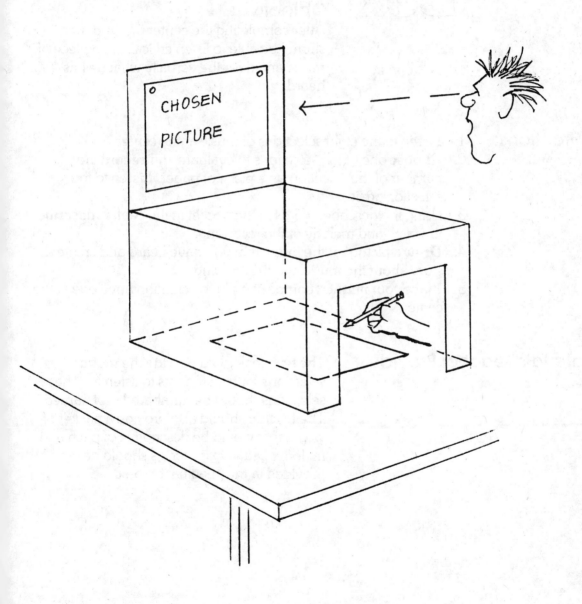

CHOSEN
PICTURE

The Music Box

Center Activity:

Objective:
After completing the center the student should be able to listen critically to a piece of music and describe verbally what he has heard.

Directions:

1. **Listen** to the eight selections of music at the center.
2. **Choose** one of the selections to evaluate and **record** the number of the selection on a piece of paper. **Listen** to the selection again.
3. Using the describer words in the packet at the center, **describe** the pitch and melody of the recording.
4. **Draw** a picture of the music that you have heard and create a story about the music and the drawing.
5. **Place** your finished composition in the creation envelope at the center.

Materials Teacher Provides:

The teacher should provide the music selections for the students to listen to. These selections should be numbered, not named. The teacher should also provide a packet of words that would be descriptive of pitch and melody. Drawing materials should be provided in the imagination box.

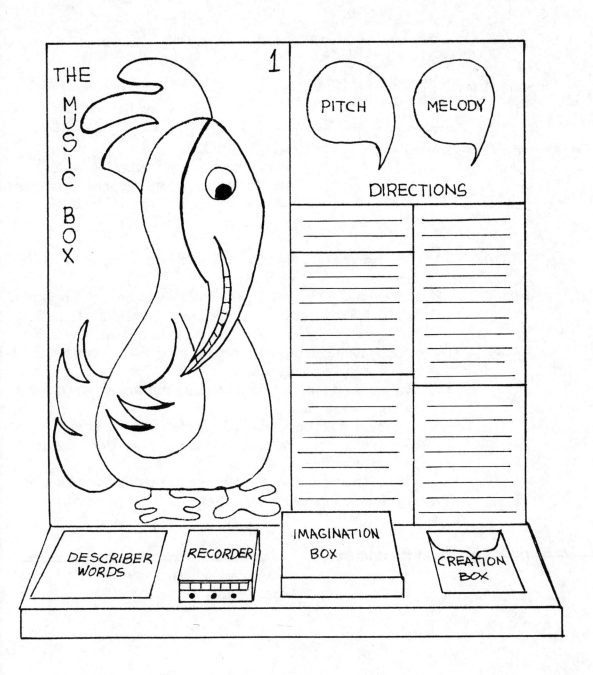

Are You Notationally Game?

Objective:

After completing the center the student should be able to correctly set up a measure of music in 2/4, 3/4, and 4/4 time.

Directions:

1. Each player **spins** the clef wheel and the time signature wheel first to set up the proper staff.
2. Players take turns spinning the note value wheel, and using the note value received they **compose** a piece of music by placing the note in the appropriate measure to be consistent with the time signature. In order to keep the note, the player must name the note and give its value.
3. The winner is the first to complete five full measures according to the time signature.
4. The music must be composed two measures at a time, so if a player spins a note value that exceeds the need for a measure, he loses that note.
5. Players should attempt to **play** their compositions on the piano after they complete five measures.

Materials Teacher Provides:

The teacher should provide staff paper, the clef and time signature spinners, and the note value spinner.

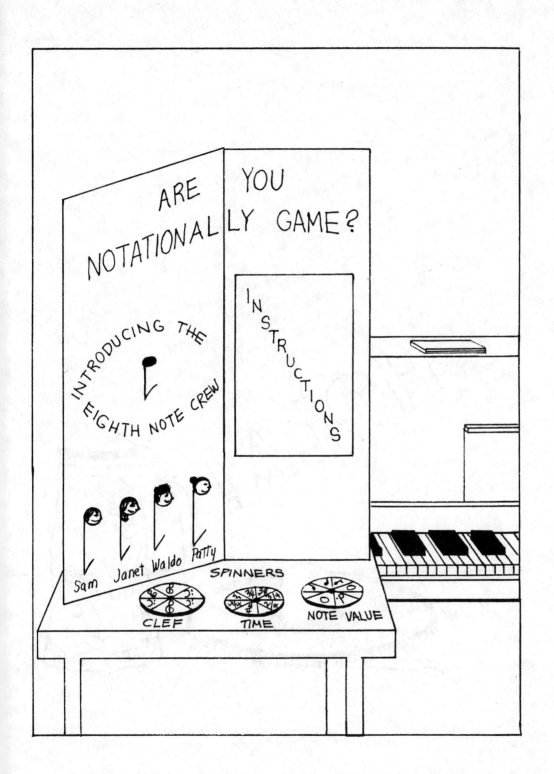

Foreign Languages

Listening- Speaking Center

Objective:

Upon completion of the center the student should be able to pronounce a phrase or expression in the language being studied and learn the equivalent expression in English.

Directions:

1. After putting on the earphones, **turn** the cassette recorder on.
2. You will first hear an expression in English, then there will be a pause when you can **say** the equivalent expression in the language studied.
3. You will then hear the correct expression in the language studied and there will be another pause for you to **repeat** the expression. Again you will hear the correct expression in the language.
4. Stop the tape at any time if you need to think before you speak. The dialogue is posted at the center, and you may follow along as you listen and speak.
5. Please **submit** your tape to your teacher upon completion.

Materials Teacher Provides:

The teacher should provide the tape of the dialogue for the student to listen to and respond on. A copy of the dialogue is usually in the textbook.

LISTENING-SPEAKING CENTER

Vocabulary Center

Objective:

After completing the center the student should be able to give the language equivalents of the vocabulary words pictured at the center.

Directions:

1. **Look** at the numbered pictures of objects and actions. Beneath each picture is a flap that conceals the correct language equivalent for the picture.
2. On your paper, **number** according to the number of pictures at the center. Beside the number of the picture, **write** the language equivalent, the masculine or feminine article if appropriate, or use the infinitive if a verb.
3. **Check** your answers by lifting the flap under each picture, and **correct** your paper.
4. **Place** your completed paper in your language folder.

Materials Teacher Provides:

The teacher should construct the center so that the pictures and answers can be changed regularly. The teacher should provide the pictures at the center with the correct language equivalent concealed under the picture.

150

Listening and Writing Center

Objective:

Upon completion of the center the student should be able to write responses in a language to questions that have been asked in that language.

Directions:

1. **Start** the tape and listen to each question.
2. **Stop** the tape after each question and *write* the answer in the language on your paper. Follow this procedure until you finish the tape.
3. **Check** your answers with the answer key provided. The answers do not need to be identical, but the general context should be the same.
4. **Place** your completed responses in your language folder.

Materials Teacher Provides:

The teacher should provide the tape recording with the questions asked. The teacher should also provide an answer key to the questions for the students to check their responses.

LISTENING and WRITING CENTER

Directions

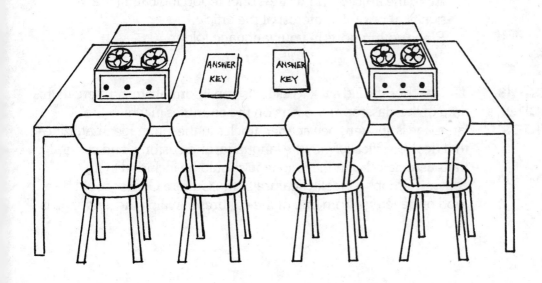

Culture Center

Objective:
Upon completion of the center the student should be able to discuss unique cultural characteristics associated with the language studied.

Directions:

1. **Select** three articles about the people and countries that speak the language being studied.
2. **Read** the articles and **write** a brief report indicating the significance or the interest of the article.
3. **Place** your reports in your language folder.

Materials Teacher Provides:

The teacher should seek to establish an informal atmosphere in this area of the classroom. Posters on the countries in which the language is spoken, newspaper articles in the language, magazines that deal specifically with the language, and customs and cultural traits associated with the language should be included in this center. Perhaps a weekly feature of the Culture Center could be a food or beverage from one of the cultures in which the language is spoken.

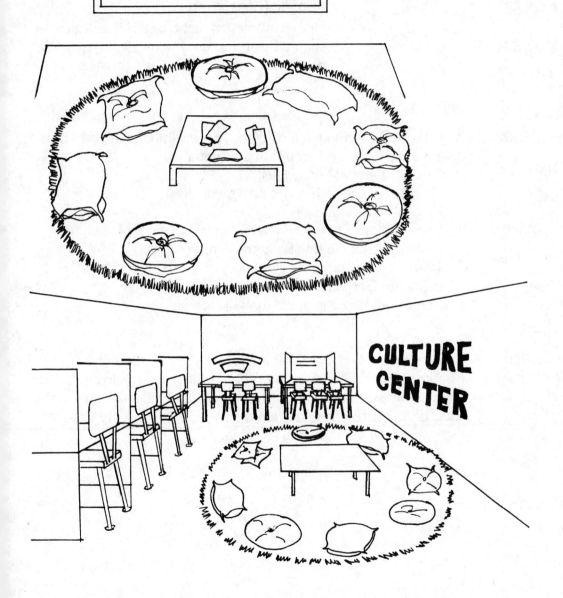

CULTURE CENTER

CULTURE CENTER

Can You Use Your Tenses?

German Center:

Objective:

Upon completion of the center the student should be able to use the present tense of the modal auxiliaries in German sentences correctly.

Directions:

1. **Examine** the conjugations of the modals listed at the center.
2. **Find** the three card groups at the center:
   Green—personal pronouns
   Orange—six conjugated modal auxiliaries
   Yellow—small phrases
3. Using the cards in the box, try to *construct* eight of the ten sentences listed in English at the center.
4. Then **choose** five of the sentences on the right and **translate** them into German.
5. **Place** your paper in your language folder.

Materials Teacher Provides:

The teacher should provide the German equivalents to the ten English sentences at the center. These sentences should be broken into personal pronouns, the six conjugated modal auxiliaries, and small phrases. The teacher should also provide the sentences for the students to translate into German.

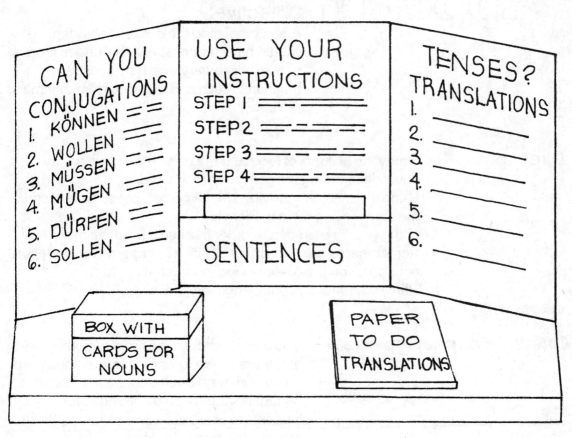

GERMAN CENTER

CAN YOU CONJUGATIONS
1. KÖNNEN
2. WOLLEN
3. MÜSSEN
4. MÜGEN
5. DÜRFEN
6. SOLLEN

USE YOUR INSTRUCTIONS
STEP 1
STEP 2
STEP 3
STEP 4

SENTENCES

TENSES?
TRANSLATIONS
1.
2.
3.
4.
5.
6.

BOX WITH CARDS FOR NOUNS

PAPER TO DO TRANSLATIONS

157

Le Repas— Bon Appétit!

Objective:
After completing the center the student should have demonstrated his understanding of new vocabulary words by constructing a menu in French and ordering from that menu on tape.

Directions:
1. **Study** the pictures of food and the French vocabulary equivalent, noting the gender of each word.
2. Using the materials provided at the center, **construct** a menu of the items, listing them in French.
3. Using your French menu, order five items from the menu. Remember to use the correct partitive in ordering food. **Record** your order on the cassette tape recorder at the center.
4. **Place** your menu in your language folder.

Materials Teacher Provides:
The teacher should construct the center so that there are pictures of common foods and the French term listed under each picture. Materials should also be provided for students to construct a French menu. Place a cassette tape recorder at the center for students to put their menu order on tape.

FRENCH CENTER

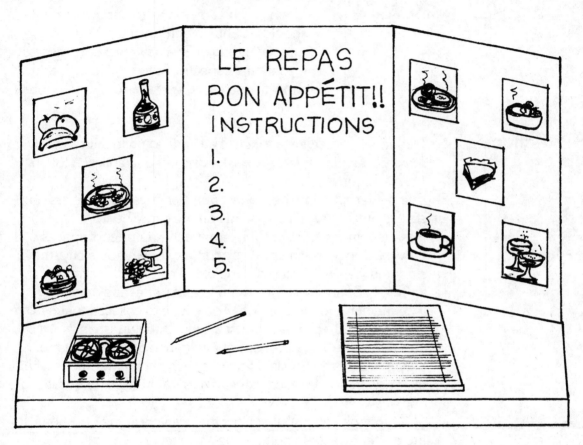

LE REPAS
BON APPÉTIT!!
INSTRUCTIONS
1.
2.
3.
4.
5.

Un Viaje Por México

Spanish Center:

Objective:

Upon completion of the center the student should be able to demonstrate an understanding of Spanish narration, discuss the cultural aspects of cities in Mexico, and show an increased verbal fluency in Spanish.

Directions:

1. Players should **select** a token. They are going to take a trip in Mexico, and the object is to visit five cities and collect a token from each one.
2. The player spinning the highest number goes first. Players can start at any of the starting points on the game board.
3. Players spin the spinner to determine the number of spaces they can move. Each time they come to or land on a city, they stop and view a filmstrip on one of the cities, with narration written in Spanish, or they listen to a cassette tape recording with the narration in Spanish. To be able to collect a token from the city visited, the player must answer three questions correctly about the city. The questions are written in Spanish, but the player answers in English. Each city has a set of questions with the answers so that each player gets a different set of questions and answers.
4. The other players should check the answers to the questions. If the player gets them right, he gets a token for that city. If he misses one of the questions, he does not get a token and must come back to the city another time for a token. The first player to get five tokens wins.

Materials Teacher Provides:

The teacher provides the game board with five or more cities in Mexico as the targets in the game. For each city there should be a short narration in Spanish about the city or a filmstrip with written Spanish narration. There should be a deck of question cards for each city with three questions about the city written in Spanish on each card and with the answers on the back of the card. A spinner with moves from 1 to 4 should be included at the game board.

5

Evaluating Learning Outcomes

Record Keeping

Record keeping in a learning center classroom does not need to be a problem. One of the easiest ways to keep records is to make an activity sheet for each unit. On the activity sheet would be listed the required centers and the product to be evaluated and the optional centers and the product or activity to be evaluated. A sample activity sheet for a learning center unit might look like:

Name of Student_____
Class Period_____
Title of Unit   The Short Story
Subject   English I-A

Name of Center and Activity	Grade	Date Completed
1. **Identifying Parts of a Short Story:** Write a report of three short stories		
2. **Famous Short Stories:** Complete the ending to a short story Make a list of authors and titles		
3. **Compare the Kinds of Conflict:** Identify kinds of conflict in three short stories		
4. **Write Your Own Short Story:** Using materials at center write an original short story		
5. Unit Examination		

UNIT GRADE_____

A key factor in the record keeping process is for both the student and the teacher to share in the responsibility. A helpful procedure for each unit is to have the student develop a unit folder. On the folder would be the title of the unit, the student's name, and any illustration the student might want to include. The top sheet inside the folder could be the prepared activity sheet indicating the learning centers and the activity or product from the center, the grade received for the work, and the date completed.

Then, when Johnny's mother and father want to know just what their son has been doing in class, the folder provides documented evidence. If the student has been doing poorly on unit or semester evaluations, the folder can be consulted to see the progress made in the centers. Notations can also be made inside the cover regarding conferences the teacher has had with the student, and the recommendations or comments from that conference can be recorded in the folder.

Conferences

Throughout a learning center approach, conferences are essential to the successful functioning of the classroom. The teacher should attempt to schedule daily conferences with students in a class during a particular period. This conference could be held during the small group sessions, as the class begins, or as the teacher works in the classroom with students at the learning centers. Within a class period, the teacher can usually schedule six to seven students for a conference. This kind of individual approach to working with students helps insure the success of the learning center program. In many classrooms, it has helped to greatly reduce the disruptive behavior of students seeking attention.

Learning Center Products

Whether the product from a learning center is a cassette tape or a written essay, the teacher needs some way of evaluating or at least acknowledging that the student has completed the assigned task. In order to keep these materials from piling up at the last minute, an easy system can be developed in which deadlines are established for the products of each center. To help in the paper shuffle or evaluation, a box can be located in a central part of the room for students to place their assignments in as they complete them daily. That way the teacher can take some assignments or products home each night to evaluate.

If the learning center has as its product a skit, panel discussion, or large group activity, a sign-up board should be kept in a central location for students to sign up for a time to make their presentations.

Many products, such as worksheets, can be placed in the unit folder so that when the final unit evaluation is made the teacher can pick up the folder, look at the activity sheet, look through the folder, record the examination grade (if one is given), and then record the unit grade on the folder. At the same time, records can be updated in the teacher's gradebook to indicate completed work.

Evaluation of learning center assignments should be a continuous process. If you find that you become overwhelmed with materials to evaluate at the end of a unit, you need to examine the procedures you are using and to establish deadlines for center materials and stick to those deadlines. The continuous aspect of learning center evaluation should make the task of evaluating learning outcomes easier, not more difficult.

Examinations

Teachers are often left with the impression that a learning center approach does not allow for necessary evaluations or tests. Although the learning center approach is designed to individualize learning, to provide for more choice in the classroom, and to encourage learners to take more responsibility for their own learning, it is not a "laissez faire" classroom methodology. Students should be just as responsible for knowing and understanding content and concepts. Although there may be many ways to determine whether a student has learned, and perhaps the testing method has been overemphasized, a learning center approach does not prevent the use of unit, semester, or yearly evaluations in terms of formal examinations.

Where examinations are used, they should be tied directly to the content and concepts presented in the learning centers and should be designed to measure the stated objectives of the centers. The unit exam should indeed tell the teacher that Johnny can perform the assigned tasks at the predetermined level. If students cannot "pass" the tests, the teacher should examine both the tests and the objectives of the unit before placing the blame on the learning center approach.

If learning center activities have been designed to foster creative thinking, value clarification, and general understanding of the subject matter, but the examination dwells on minutiae or memorized facts, then it is not the process at fault but the procedure of evaluation and the structuring of the centers.

Content material that deals with specific details, terms, or facts has a definite place in the learning center approach and in an evaluation procedure. However, the learning center approach is often a dismal failure because instead of presenting a variety of activities and learning opportunities, the center creators put the same old procedures of read the chapter, define the terms at the end, and answer the questions for discussion in new clothing without the necessary motivational alternative activities.

6

After Learning Centers, Then What?

Student-Made Learning Centers

One of the greatest things to happen in classrooms that use the learning center approach is that students want to begin to design their own learning centers. Teams of students can even be established to work up the learning centers for the next unit, with the teacher or team of teachers serving as resource people. This outcome does not mean that the teacher loses control of what is being taught but simply that the teacher has students helping develop the material that will be used to teach the unit. What more could any teacher want?

Student-made learning centers can be the most challenging to other students. They typically involve much more than the teacher would include because the students become so motivated that they want to include everything about the topic to be studied. The team that plans the learning center activities not only has to participate in them but can serve as peer tutors to other students in the classroom.

A good way to establish teams to work on the next unit is to involve both the students who are having trouble with learning the material and the students who are always seeking more information. Both ranges of student abilities should be included in the planning process.

One of the rewards of student-made learning centers is that they provide the teacher with the opportunity to work with students in a different role while at the same time releasing part of the time-consuming responsibility of actually constructing the learning centers.

Projects for Groups and Individuals

Topics at the learning centers often spawn ideas for group and individual projects that could be completed during the reporting period or the school term. The topics may capitalize on a particular student interest and students will want to do more.

After learning centers comes a more rewarding involvement in seeing students either individually or in small groups pursue a topic because they really want to know more about it. One student that participated in the short story unit became so interested in the short story, particularly the one he wrote, that he kept polishing it up and rewriting it until he submitted it to several magazines and finally saw it published.

Independent Study

In conjunction with the projects that arise from the use of learning centers, many students will wish to pursue an independent study program. Such a desire can often be met by establishing a contractual agreement with the student about the nature of the study and the kinds of activities to be done in connection with the independent study.

One student became so involved with the study of animal anatomy that he was considering a career in veterinary medicine. As a part of his independent study program, he made several field trips to an animal clinic to talk with the veterinarian. He also visited a school of veterinary medicine to learn about the process of becoming an animal doctor. The product of this independent study was a report to the class and a slide preparation entitled "A Dog's Best Friend — The Vet."

One of the purposes of the learning center approach is to stimulate such an interest in students. This purpose is not unique to learning centers; however, the learning center approach, with its emphasis on student responsibility and choice, encourages such processes as independent study.